Table of Contents

MW01613729

Introduction: Safety First

Water and electricity don't mix. Consult or hire an electrician instead of doing any electrical work. Electricity can kill.

Always proceed with caution, and use personal protection equipment. Be aware of your surroundings when performing an inspection, especially when there are electrical components and water in close proximity to each other.

Never grab wires or components without disconnecting them from their power source. Wear rubber-soled shoes and rubber gloves. Don't stand in water when working with or inspecting equipment. Be sure to identify all circuits that are related to the pool equipment. When inspecting the pool or spa, check for unfinished or poor workmanship, particularly with the electrical components, wiring and installation.

If you are doing a visual-only inspection, stick to using your eyes only and not your hands. Don't open anything that you're not required to open, especially electrical components, boxes and panels.

Check grounding wire connections, loose wires and conduits, and water leaks. Remember that water is an effective conductor of electricity. If there is an electrical problem with the pool equipment, a fault could occur and charge the entire pool or spa, making it fatally hazardous. Be careful.

This Book Is a Companion Study Guide to the Online Course:

How to Inspect Pools & Spas

InterNACHI Members: Take the free, online *How to Inspect Pools & Spas* course now (free to InterNACHI members)

The course is free for all InterNACHI® members.

Upon successfully completing the online course and passing the final exam, you will receive a Certificate of Completion and be able to:

- inspect the systems and components of residential pools and spas for proper functionality;

- identify safety issues; and

- provide your clients with accurate and useful information, including a list of common maintenance recommendations.

Take the online course at **www.nachi.org/pool-spa-course**

How to Inspect Pools & Spas

The purpose of this publication is to provide accurate and useful information for home inspectors in order to perform an inspection of pools and spas at residential properties. This manual covers the following topics: how pools and spas work; the circulation, heating and filtering systems and components; the electrical components; water chemistry; safety issues; maintenance recommendations; and an inspection procedural checklist. The focus of this book and its corresponding online course is on the water of residential pools and spas, and the systems and components that move or change it. This publication is a useful tool as a portable guide for inspectors on the job. It also serves as a study aid for InterNACHI's online *How to Inspect Pools and Spas* course and exam.

To order additional training books, visit www.InspectorOutlet.com

Authors:

Ben Gromicko, Director of Education
Nick Gromicko, Founder

Graphics:

Lisaira Vega, Wylie Robinson, Levi Nelson, Jackson Tupper & Erica Saurey

Editor:

Kate Tarasenko / Crimea River, LLC

Layout & Design:

Jessica Langer

www.NACHI.org

Section 1: The Basics

Swimming Pool and Spa

For purposes of this guide, a swimming pool is considered a permanent structure in the ground, or partially in the ground, that is capable of holding water with a depth greater than 42 inches outside a building, as well as all pools installed inside a building without regard to water depth.

The terms "spa" and "hot tub" are used here interchangeably. A spa or hot tub is a hydro-massage pool or tub used for recreational or therapeutic use, not located in a healthcare facility. They typically use a filter, heater and motor-driven blower. A hot tub is usually built with wood. A spa is usually made with fiberglass.

POOL & SPA PLUMBING LAYOUT

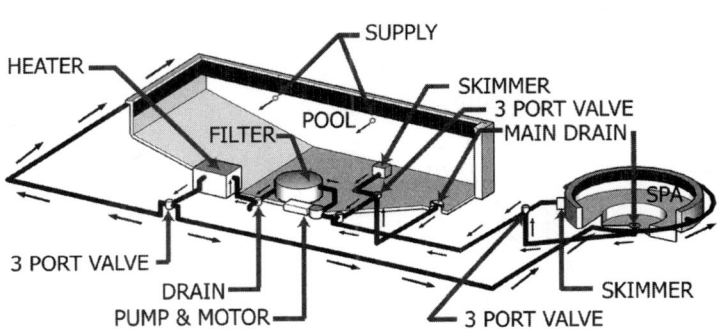

This is an illustration of a typical pool and spa with its components moving water through the systems. A hot tub or spa moves and changes water in a way similar to that of a pool. They share the same type of plumbing, electrical and maintenance requirements. To understand how a pool or spa works, you should follow the path of the water. In a pool or spa, water flows from the container (pool or spa) through the plumbing, to the pump, filter and heating system, and then returns to the container.

This guide is outlined in a similar fashion—by following the path of the water. Let's first look at the flow of water.

In the illustration, the arrows indicate the flow of water through the pool and spa. Starting with the water inside the container, the water exits the container through the main drain and/or surface skimmer. The pump sucks the water out of the container through the drain and/or skimmer, and then pushes the water through the rest of the system. The water travels from the container through the pump, through the filter (where it is cleaned), through the heater (where it is heated), and then returns to the container.

How Big Is It?

Calculating the amount of water that the pool or hot tub holds is useful to know how to do for maintaining and servicing the pool, for adding chemicals to the water, and for draining and filling the container.

Square or Rectangular

If the pool is square or rectangular, the equation to calculate how much water is in the pool is fairly simple.

The volume of the water, in gallons, inside a pool or spa equals the length multiplied by the width multiplied by the average depth multiplied by 7.5, like this:

Volume (gallons) = length x width x average depth x 7.5.

To determine the volume, you could measure the length of the rectangular pool, then measure the width, and then the depth of the pool. That will give you the volume in cubic feet of water.

Since there are 7.5 gallons of water in 1 cubic foot of water, multiply the volume by 7.5 to get the volume expressed in gallons.

What if you measure one dimension and it's a fraction of a foot? Multiply the inches by 0.08333 to get a percentage of a foot. For example, let's say you measured the width to be 12 feet and 3 inches. Multiply the 3 by 0.0833 to arrive at a fraction that is easy to work with, like this: 3 x 0.0833 = 0.25. The width in the example would be 12.25 feet.

If you need to measure in meters, the equation works the same:

length x width x average depth = volume in cubic meters.

Since there are 1,000 liters in 1 cubic meter, then the equation becomes:

length x width x average depth x 1,000 = volume in liters.

If you are measuring a pool that is deep in one end and shallow in the other but does not have a gradual slope, then measuring volume may involve breaking up the pool into parts, calculating, and adding them together.

Measuring a container in parts is typically required when you have a spa or hot tub. Spas and hot tub containers have seats, bumpouts and compartments. Typically, there is no water under the seats. You have to break up the hot tub into at least two calculations. Some styles of hot tubs made of wood have circulating water under the seats but that's uncommon.

It is important to remember that the volume of the container is a bigger number than you need. If you are measuring how much water the container holds while being used, then you must be aware of the actual water depth. The actual water depth of the pool is not the same as the depth of the pool. In a typical hot tub, the water is filled to only about three-quarters of the way.

Circular

If the container is circular, then use the following equation to determine the volume of water in the container:

pi x r² x average depth x 7.5 = volume in gallons.

Pi (π) is a mathematical constant that equals 3.14. The "r" is the radius. The radius is the measurement that is one-half of the diameter of the circle. The diameter is the straight line across the middle of the circle. Radius² is simply the radius multiplied by itself (radius x radius = radius²). If you want to measure in liters, then use 1,000 instead of 7.5.

For example, if the hot tub is 6 feet across the middle, which is its diameter, the radius is 3 feet. Radius² equals 9 (3 x 3).

Irregular

If the pool or spa is irregular in shape, then you'll have to do some additional calculations and adding of parts. You have to imagine the pool or spa as a combination of smaller, regular shapes. Measure those areas, make your volume calculations for each, then add them all together.

Parts per Million

To understand how much chemicals are added to the pool or spa, you need to understand the term "parts per million," or ppm. Parts-per is used when measuring the amount of solids that exist in a liquid. So, "1 ppm" means one part mixed with a million parts.

Three parts of chlorine that exist in every 1 million parts of water can be expressed as 3 ppm. However, 3 *gallons* of chlorine chemicals added to 1 million gallons of pool water does not translate as 3 ppm. That is because the two are not the same. Chlorine liquid does not have the same density as pool water. Chlorine liquid, which weighs 10 pounds per gallon, is heavier than pool water, which weighs 8.3 pounds per gallon. Chlorine is denser than water. There's actually more of it relative to an equal volume of water.

So, to add chlorine to a pool of water, you first have to translate the amounts of the two liquids so that they're expressed as pounds. You have to express the amount of chlorine in pounds, and you have to express the amount of water in pounds. One gallon of chlorine weighs 10 pounds. One gallon of water weighs 8.3 pounds. Then you have to translate that to parts of chlorine per 1 million parts of water. And then it gets even more complicated when you realize that a bucket of chlorine comes in a 10% to 15% solution, meaning that 10% to 15% of what comes out of the bucket or bottle is chlorine, and the rest is inert ingredients or filler.

It is very important to be able to measure the volume of the pool or spa and the amount of chemicals being added to the water. It is difficult to do, but essential to know.

By the way, 1 part per trillion (1 ppt) is a proportion equivalent to 1/20 of a drop of water diluted into a 2-meter-deep, Olympic-size swimming pool.

Quiz 1

1. A swimming pool is a permanent structure in the ground, or partially in the ground, that is capable of holding water with a depth greater than _____ inches outside a building.

     ☐ 62

     ☐ 42

     ☐ 22

2. T/F: A hot tub or spa moves and changes water in way similar to that of a pool.

     ☐ True

     ☐ False

3. There are _____ gallons of water in 1 cubic foot of water.

     ☐ 3

     ☐ 4.2

     ☐ 7.5

     ☐ 9.8

4. T/F: "1 ppm" means one part mixed with a million parts.

     ☐ True

     ☐ False

5. One gallon of water weighs _____ pounds.

     ☐ 2

     ☐ 7.2

     ☐ 8.3

     ☐ 10.4

Answer Key is on page 83.

Section 2:
InterNACHI's Pool & Spa Inspection Standards of Practice

InterNACHI's Residential Pool and Spa Inspection Standards of Practice includes the following:

1. Definitions and Scope

2. Limitations, Exceptions and Exclusions

3. Residential Pool and Spa Inspection

4. Glossary of Terms

1. Definitions and Scope

1.1. A **residential pool and spa inspection** is a non-invasive, visual examination of the accessible areas of a pool or spa (as delineated below), performed for a fee, which is designed to identify defects within specific systems and components defined by these Standards that are both observed and deemed material by the inspector. The scope of work may be modified by the Client and Inspector prior to the inspection process.

> I. The residential pool and spa inspection is based on the observations made on the date of the inspection, and not a prediction of future conditions.

> II. The residential pool and spa inspection will not reveal every issue that exists or ever could exist, but only those material defects observed on the date of the inspection.

1.2. A **material defect** is a specific issue with a system or component that may have a significant, adverse impact on the value of the property, or that poses an unreasonable risk to people. The fact that a system or component is near, at, or beyond the end of its normal, useful life is not, in itself, a material defect.

1.3. A **residential pool and spa inspection report** shall identify, in written format, defects within specific systems and components defined by these Standards that are both observed and deemed material by the inspector. Residential pool and spa inspection reports may also provide causes for these defects and possible future options that may include remediation or further evaluation. Residential pool and spa inspection reports may include additional comments and recommendations.

> I. The inspector is not required to inspect or perform any action not explicitly detailed in these Standards.

2. Limitations, Exceptions and Exclusions

2.1. Limitations:

> I. The inspector is not required to inspect or perform any action not explicitly detailed in these Standards.

> II. The inspector is not required to come into direct contact with pool or spa water.

> III. The inspector is not required to enter the pool or spa.

IV. The inspector is not required to drain a pool or spa in order to inspect it.

V. A residential pool and spa inspection is not technically exhaustive.

VI. A residential pool and spa inspection will not identify concealed or latent defects.

VII. A residential pool and spa inspection will not deal with aesthetic concerns, or what could be deemed matters of taste, cosmetic defects, etc.

VIII. A residential pool and spa inspection does not include items not permanently installed.

2.2. Exclusions:

I. The inspector is not required to determine:

A. the condition of any component or system that is not readily accessible.

B. the service life expectancy of any component or system.

C. the size, capacity, performance or efficiency of any component or system.

D. the cause or reason of any condition.

E. the cause for the need of correction, repair or replacement of any system or component.

F. future conditions.

G. compliance with codes or regulations.

H. the presence of evidence of rodents, birds, bats, animals, insects, or other pests.

I. the presence of mold, mildew or fungus.

J. the existence of environmental hazards.

K. the existence of electromagnetic fields.

L. any hazardous waste conditions.

M. any manufacturers' recalls or conformance with manufacturer installation, or any information included for consumer protection purposes.

N. correction, replacement or repair cost estimates.

O. estimates of the cost to operate any given system.

II. The inspector is not required to operate:

A. any system that is shut down.

B. any system that does not function properly.

C. any system that does not turn on with the use of normal operating controls.

D. any shut-off valves or manual stop valves.

E. any electrical disconnect or over-current protection devices.

F. any alarm systems.

III. The inspector is not required to:

A. perform any action that contradicts any laws or regulations.

B. activate any component of the pool or spa.

C. move any personal items or other obstructions, such as, but not limited to: furniture, equipment or debris.

D. dismantle, open or uncover any system or component.

E. enter or access any area that may, in the inspector's opinion, be unsafe.

F. do anything that may, in the inspector's opinion, be unsafe or dangerous to him/herself or others, or damage property, such as, but not limited to negotiating with pets.

G. inspect decorative items.

H. offer guarantees or warranties.

I. offer or perform any engineering services.

J. offer or perform any trade or professional service other than a pool and spa inspection.

K. research the history of the property, or report on its potential for alteration, modification, extendibility or suitability for a specific or proposed use for occupancy.

L. determine the age of construction or installation of any system, structure or component of a unit, or differentiate between original construction and subsequent additions, improvements, renovations or replacements.

M. determine the insurability of the property.

3. Residential Pool and Spa Inspection

I. The inspector shall inspect from ground level:

A. the plumbing;

B. the filters;

C. the lights;

D. any adjoining structure as it relates to the pool or spa;

E. the valves;

F. the solar heating system;

G. the pumps and motors;

H. the electrical system;

I. the filtration system;

J. the pool heater; and

K. the safety barriers.

II. The inspector shall describe:

A. the type of swimming pool or spa;

B. details impacting the inspector's ability to inspect the unit, including water clarity;

C. the condition of visible components or systems present in the unit;

D. the type of drain installed;

E. any readily accessible component with functional or material defects;

F. the type of filtration system; and

G. the types of safety barriers.

III. The inspector shall report as in need of correction:

> A. observed indications of active pool or spa shell leaks;
>
> B. damaged water line tiles;
>
> C. damaged or faulty drain covers, pumps; heaters or filter housings;
>
> D. inadequate drainage;
>
> E. Improper settlement of pool deck; and
>
> F. any visibly unsafe or improper pool equipment, electrical connections, or bonding connections.

4. Glossary of Terms

- **accessible:** In the opinion of the inspector, can be approached or entered safely, without difficulty, fear or danger.

- **activate:** To turn on, supply power, or enable systems, equipment or devices to become active by normal operating controls.

- **adverse effect:** Refers to anything that may constitute, or potentially constitute, a negative or destructive impact.

- **alarm system:** Warning devices, installed or freestanding, including, but not limited to, spillage detectors.

- **component:** A permanently installed or attached fixture, element or part of a system.

- **condition:** The visible and conspicuous state of being of an object.

- **correction:** Something that is substituted or proposed for what is incorrect, deficient, unsafe, or a defect.

- **cosmetic defect:** An irregularity or imperfection in something that could be corrected, but is not required to be.

- **decorative:** Ornamental; not required for the operation of essential systems or components.

- **describe:** To report in writing a system or component by its type or other observed characteristics in order to distinguish it from other components used for the same purpose.

- **determine:** To arrive at an opinion or conclusion pursuant to examination.

- **dismantle:** To open, take apart or remove any component, device or piece that would not typically be opened, taken apart or removed by an ordinary occupant.

- **engineering service:** Any professional service or creative work requiring engineering education, training and experience, and the application of special knowledge of the mathematical, physical and engineering sciences to such professional service or creative work as consultation, investigation, evaluation, planning, design and supervision of construction for the purpose of assuring compliance with the specifications and design, in conjunction with structures, buildings, machines, equipment, works and/or processes.

- **enter:** To go into an area to observe visible components.

- **evaluate:** To assess the systems, structures and/or components.

- **evidence:** That which tends to prove or disprove something; something that makes plain or clear; grounds for belief; proof.

- **examine:** To visually look (see **inspect**).

- **function:** The action for which an item, component or system is specially fitted or used, or for which an item, component or system exists; to be in action or perform a task.

- **functional:** Performing, or able to perform, a function.

- **functional defect:** A lack of or an abnormality in something that is necessary for normal and proper functioning and operation, and, therefore, requires further evaluation and correction.

- **identify:** To notice and report.

- **indication:** That which serves to point out, show, or make known the present existence of something under certain conditions.

- **inspect:** To examine readily accessible systems and components safely, using normal operating controls, and accessing readily accessible areas, in accordance with these Standards of Practice.

- **inspection report:** A written communication (possibly including images) of any material defects observed during the inspection.

- **inspector:** One who performs an inspection.

- **installed:** Attached or connected such that the installed item requires a tool for removal.

- **material defect:** A specific issue with a system or component that may have a significant, adverse impact on the value of the property, or that poses an unreasonable risk to people. The fact that a system or component is near, at, or beyond the end of its normal, useful life is not, in itself, a material defect.

- **normal operating controls:** Describes the method by which certain devices (such as thermostats) can be operated by ordinary occupants, as they require no specialized skill or knowledge.

- **observe:** To visually notice.

- **operate:** To cause systems to function or turn on with normal operating controls.

- **readily accessible:** A system or component that, in the judgment of the inspector, is capable of being safely observed without the removal of obstacles, detachment or disengagement of connecting or securing devices, or other unsafe or difficult procedures to gain access.

- **report (verb form):** To express, communicate or provide information in writing; give a written account of. (See also **inspection report.**)

- **shut down:** Turned off, unplugged, inactive, not in service, not operational, etc.

- **system:** An assembly of various components which function as a whole.

- **technically exhaustive:** A comprehensive and detailed examination beyond the scope of an inspection that would involve or include, but would not be limited to: dismantling, specialized knowledge or training, special equipment, measurements, calculations, testing, research, analysis, or other means.

- **unsafe:** In the inspector's opinion, a condition of an area, system, component or procedure that is judged to be a significant risk of injury during normal, day-to-day use. The risk may be due to damage, deterioration, improper installation, or a change in accepted residential construction standards.

Section 3: Types of Pools & Spas

Concrete

The most common in-ground pool is made of concrete. Plaster or fiberglass might line the concrete. Reinforced concrete is used to form the shell (the walls and floor). The concrete surface can be coated with plaster to keep the porous material from absorbing or leaking water. The plaster holds the water in, and it also makes the concrete look nice. Fiberglass is popular, too, because it requires less maintenance than plaster. Pool installers commonly spray the concrete over the steel reinforcement bars (rebar). They can also pour the concrete into forms. "Gunite" refers to the result of a dry-mix process in which the dry, cementitious mixture is blown from a pressure "gun" through a hose, where water is injected immediately before application. "Shotcrete" results from a wet-mix process in which the cementitious mixture is also blown from a gun, but it's wetter. If a spa is designed and built on-site as a custom unit, then it is typically made of concrete.

Spas are commonly installed as a fully-equipped unit made with a fiberglass or acrylic shell and a wooden skirt.

Vinyl-Lined

Vinyl Lined Pools

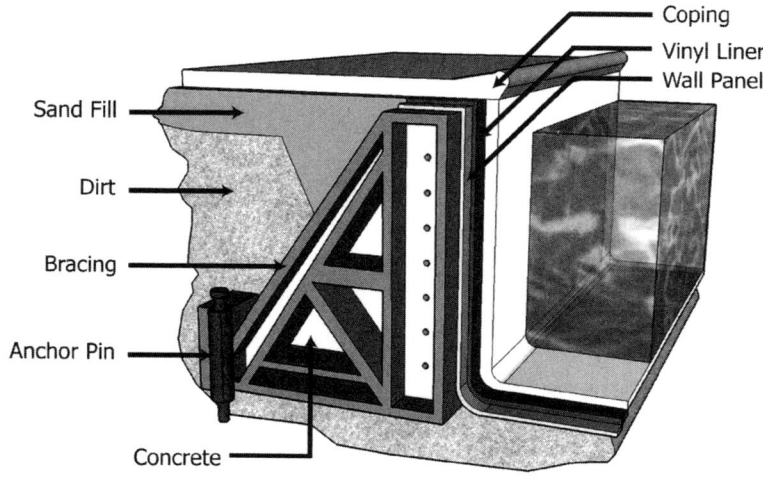

Sand Fill
Dirt
Bracing
Anchor Pin
Concrete

Coping
Vinyl Liner
Wall Panel

Vinyl-lined pools are installed above the ground or set in the ground. The pool frame (the structural walls of the pool) is made of prefabricated panels of aluminum, plastic, steel or wood. The panels are secured to the ground and attached to each other. Steel walls are durable; they withstand expansion and contraction in freezing climates. And steel is the least expensive. The walls are then lined with heavy vinyl. This vinyl material is waterproof and holds the water. Installation is easier and less expensive than a concrete pool. But steel panels corrode; look for rust and corrosion if the panel material is readily visible.

Fiberglass

Fiberglass pools can be above the ground or set in the ground. Above-ground fiberglass pools have metal or plastic frame construction. Some concrete pools are lined with fiberglass instead of plaster or vinyl. Most spas are made of fiberglass or acrylic, unless they are designed and built on-site. Fiberglass spas can be set into the ground, or they can be freestanding units with their own frame support with a wooden skirt around the unit. The fiberglass spa unit typically contains all of the equipment in one package.

Above-Ground

There are many different types of pools and spas that can be installed above the ground. Above-ground pools are more affordable than in-ground pools. Many are portable and can be put away when cold weather arrives. Most above-ground pools are not designed to be buried, and doing so could cause the pool to collapse inward. Consult the manufacturer's recommendations or installation manual to determine the specific guidelines for the pool. An above-ground pool should not be positioned on or near a septic system. The above-ground pool should be level within 1 inch. Unlevel installation places extreme forces on the pool and may cause it to deform or fail.

Wood

Some pools and spas are made of wood, but they are not common. Redwood is the most popular choice of wood, but other woods can be used, too, such as cedar and teak. Hot tub seats and skirts are usually made of wood.

Construction Process

There is a general, step-by-step procedure that is followed when a pool is built. First, an architect or pool contractor examines the site and designs the pool, which might include inspecting the ground's geology and soil stability. Permits must be approved before any construction takes place. Then comes the excavation based on the plans. The excavator digs out the pool and trenches for pipes and equipment. Gravel is added into the finished hole. The plumbing and steel work are installed. The main drain is installed. Skimmers are put in place, usually where the prevailing wind will push debris toward them. After all the plumbing is installed, it is tested under pressure for leaks. The steel and rebar are installed. Rebar is criss-crossed all over the contoured design of the pool.

Swimming Pool - Tile and Concrete Work

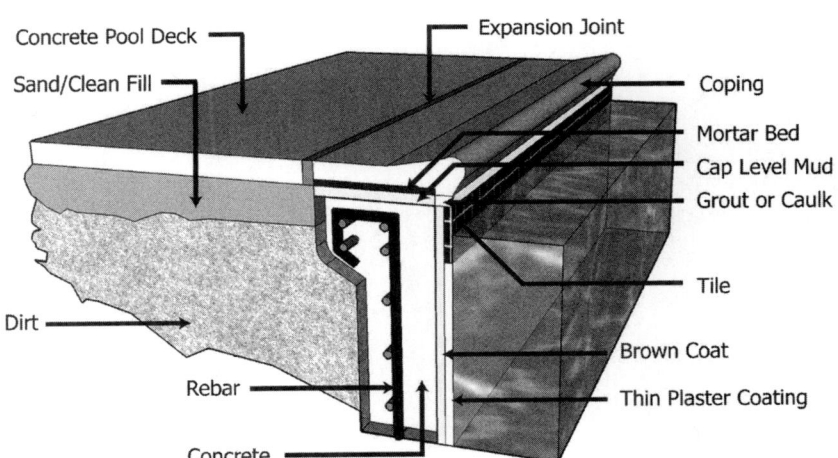

The top part of the pool wall is reinforced with heavy steel. It is called the bond beam, which supports the coping and edge around the pool. An electrician grounds or bonds the steel of the pool to the earth. All of the electrical components are installed, including light fixtures. Gunite or shotcrete is blown into the pool or spa. The thickness of the concrete is typically around 5 inches for the walls, around 6 inches for the floor, and 10 inches for the bond beam. Tile is then installed, usually around the waterline. Tile is not porous and can be easily cleaned. The entire pool can be tiled, which is costly but can be easier to maintain.

Rocks and stone can be installed for aesthetic reasons. Real stone can be installed but, more often, artificial rocks are used, shaped on-site with light rebar and cementitious concrete. Natural rock often develops a white scale at the waterline caused by minerals left behind after natural evaporation occurs.

Coping is the finish work done at the bond-beam area, which is the top of the walls of the pool or spa. Coping stones and tiles are made of porous materials to provide a non-slip surface for swimmers. Then comes the deck or walks around the pool.

Stone, wood and brick are commonly used for the decks, steps, seats and walks surrounding pools and spas.

A ¼- to ½-inch gap is left between the coping and the surrounding material, a provision for expansion and contraction of the deck and coping materials in hot and cold climates. Gaps, separations and openings of all kinds and in all areas are then sealed up with silicone caulking to keep water out.

The pool equipment is then installed, including the pump, filter and heating system. Plaster might be troweled over the concrete. The pool surface plaster can be of any color, though it is usually white.

Water is then added to the pool. The plaster can harden and cure underwater.

Quiz 2

1. The most common in-ground pool shell is made of _____.

    ☐ fiberglass

    ☐ plastic

    ☐ concrete

    ☐ tile

2. Most _____ are made of fiberglass or acrylic, unless they are designed and built on-site.

    ☐ pools

    ☐ spas

3. An above-ground pool should be level within _____.

    ☐ 1/2-inch

    ☐ 1 inch

    ☐ 6 inches

    ☐ 1 foot

4. The top part of a pool wall is called the _____, which supports the coping and edge around the pool.

    ☐ cope stock

    ☐ I-beam

    ☐ bond beam

    ☐ parapet

5. T/F: The pool's surface plaster cannot be of any color other than white.

    ☐ True

    ☐ False

Answer Key is on page 83.

Section 4: Plumbing

Following the Path of the Water

To understand how a pool or spa works, you can follow the path that the water takes in a pool or spa system. The pool container holds the water. The water is sucked out of the container through the main drain on the floor, through a skimmer, or through a combination of the two. Then, it might go through a special valve called a three-port valve, and then into the pump. The pump pushes the water through the filter and the heating system (which might include solar panels). The water then returns to the pool or spa through the return lines and ports.

The circulation system is generally one of two designs: direct suction or overflow. Direct suction means the pump is sucking water from the main drain and/or return outlets. Overflow means that there's a displacement of water from bathers that is caught in the gutter, skimmer systems, or collection tank. Overflow systems typically incorporate a gutter system at a commercial pool installation.

POOL & SPA PLUMBING LAYOUT

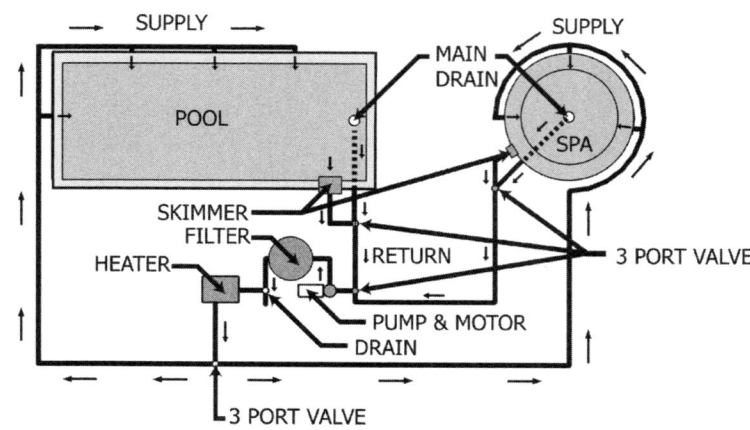

Main Drains

Main drains are usually located at the deepest part of a pool. Water is sucked through the drain to the pump and circulated through the system. There is typically one main drain for a residential in-ground pool, and that main drain usually has one port that feeds a pipe to the pump.

When the pump is on, water is sucked from the pool through the main drain and skimmer. Inside a spa or hot tub, there might be several ports feeding pipes to different pumps that make different types of water jet action.

There should be no changes to the main drain's size or location unless it is evaluated by the engineer or pool expert who designed the installation.

The main drain, which is located on the pool floor, might have a special hydrostatic port. This type of port is a one-way port that allows water that collects underneath the pool floor to enter the drain, which prevents water from leaking out of the pool. If water collects underneath a pool, extreme upward pressure may be created that could crack the pool. This pressure is called hydrostatic pressure.

In some pools and spas, there might be more than one main drain. If one drain is clogged or blocked by a hand or foot, the other will be open and water can be pulled from that drain instead. This helps prevent injuring the person who is blocking the main drain. If the main drain is located on a pool floor that is very deep, this safety suction line might not be necessary. At any pool, there should be a balance of suction at the main drain and the skimmer to prevent injuring someone who might be blocking a port.

Some drains can cause a whirlpool effect. For these drains, which are typically located in shallow pools, a special domed cover could be installed at the main drain to prevent this action. Otherwise, the main drain at the deep end of the pool will have a grate installed on it. The cover might be flat with grated openings. The drain is usually 6 to 12 inches in diameter.

The main drain should be visually inspected regularly (ideally, daily), particularly when the pool is being serviced or when the pool floor is being swept. There shouldn't be any damage, clogging or cracks at the drain cover.

It is important to minimize the flow through the main drain to prevent entrapment problems. Local codes regulate the water flow rates through the system.

Skimmers

The highest concentration of contamination is located at the surface of the pool. Airborne debris, algae, bodily discharge, oils, etc., all float to the surface. The pool's disinfection level is typically lowest at the surface. It is important that part of the circulation and filtration process includes skimming the surface of the water. The highest percentage of the circulation process should include the surface water. A common practice is to have 75% of the water from the surface removed.

Skimmers are box-like openings in the wall of the pool located at the surface of the water. Some pool codes require one skimmer for every 500 square feet of surface water.

Skimmers are vented to the atmosphere, typically through the "finger holes" in the lid.

A pool can have one or more skimmers. A skimmer skims the surface of the pool and cleans it by sucking water that is on the surface into the system. It pulls in leaves, debris, bugs and dirt before all that stuff falls to the bottom of the pool. A skimmer can vacuum a pool by attaching a hose or suction line.

The skimmer basket is the first step in filtering debris. The basket captures large debris and leaves before they enter the system. The skimmer basket should be cleaned of any debris that is collected daily. To empty the skimmer basket, the lid or cover has to be opened. The basket should be removed, emptied and returned. The skimmer's cover needs to be secured back in place. Maintaining the skimmer basket increases the efficiency with which water circulates through the system, and keeps the pool clean.

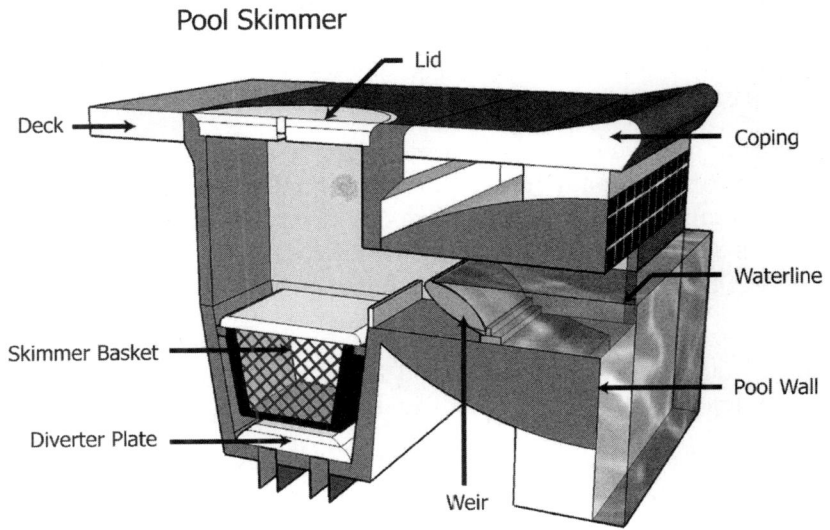

Pool Skimmer

A typical skimmer has a weir, which is the small floating, hinged device that allows water to enter the skimmer. The floating weir will always adjust to the level of the water and provides the skimming action. When the suction stops and water stops entering the skimmer basket, the floating weir rises up and prevents debris from coming out of the skimmer and re-entering the pool.

Weirs can cause problems if they stick closed (or in the upright position), thus blocking water from entering the system. If water is blocked from entering, the pump will lose prime (or water flow) and will run dry, causing damage.

Pumps are not designed to run without water or run dry for more than a few minutes while priming. For this reason, not all skimmers have weirs.

There's typically an access cover above the skimmer. Most covers for skimmers are built into the walking surface or deck area surrounding the pool.

Some skimmers are separate and not directly integrated with the plumbing system. Portable and above-ground pools commonly use separate skimmers that attach and overhang the side of the pool.

Be sure to keep away from the skimmer when the pump is on. Skimmers have been known to pull on fingers, shirts and small objects. Keep your hands from covering the pipe's suction hole inside the skimmer.

At each skimmer, there are two pipes. One pipe comes from the main drain. The other pipe goes to the pump. There are two general types of skimmer plumbing. The first type has one visible opening. The other might have two.

Most skimmers have a design feature that can be used to adjust the flow of water that passes through them, allowing multiple units to work together effectively in providing good circulation of the water's surface.

Inside the single-opening skimmer, you will see a single opening or port. The water from the pool's surface is sucked into that opening. Below that opening is a connection of both the pump and the main drainpipes. A combination diverter is inserted into the opening to control the amount of water that flows from either the main drain or the skimmer. Imagine that the pump is on and sucking on the pipe that goes to the skimmer. It's also sucking on the pipe that goes to the main drain at the pool floor. At the skimmer is where the two pipes connect. At that connection, there's a diverter device that can be adjusted to control the amount of suction that comes from the main drain and skimmer. Adjust it one way and you can have a lot of suction coming from the drain at the pool floor. And that's good when you have a pool with a lot of dirt instead of floating leaves. Adjust it the other way and you have a lot of suction coming from the skimmer. And that's good when you have a pool with a lot of floating leaves.

The other type of skimmer has two pipes (or port openings) with a plate on top of the openings that regulates the suction between the main drain and the skimmer. Another type of skimmer has an equalizer line, which is simply a pipe that goes from the skimmer downward to an exit hole through the pool wall below the skimmer. The idea is to prevent the pump from running dry. The pump should always have water flowing to it, and that type of control can be found at the skimmer.

These diverter fittings are usually made of plastic. They often break or fall out of the skimmer. Plastic diverters tend to rotate when vacuuming, and that could be a problem when adjusting the suction between skimmers and main drains. Bronze diverters are optimal.

When you attach a pool vacuum hose to the opening port inside the skimmer, water can be blocked from the main drain at the pool floor, and most of the suction will go to the hose. A wall vacuum-cleaner fitting can be installed in the pool wall, typically located 6 to 18 inches below the pool's water level.

Each pool can be adjusted to compensate for various factors, such as wind, equipment efficiency, and the type of cleaning being performed.

When visually inspecting the skimmer, look for any cracks in the material, a missing basket, or a broken gasket. Be sure to inspect the inside of the mouth of the skimmer, as this area is prone to breaking. Indications of repair, glue, epoxy or cracks should be reported. Skimmers should not have visible repairs. Repairs will likely not be reliable. A crack in the skimmer might allow the pool to leak. If the pool is leaking, there may be a crack or separation that is allowing water to leak out of the pool through the skimmer unit. Replacement is typically recommended, but that requires a much larger undertaking and might involve working with a new liner or plaster work.

Gutters

Gutters are typically found in commercial pool installations. There are different types, including scum, surge and rim-flow. Gutters are similar to troughs that work by the principle of surface tension pulling the water into the gutter. The top layer of the pool water is drawn into the gutter system. Surge gutters are designed to handle a large volume of water and are found at large private and public pools. Gutters have grates above them that can be walked upon.

Suction and Entrapment

Circulating the water in a pool can create a risk to bathers, who can be entrapped in the vacuum flow created by the pump. Once trapped, a person can be injured or drowned.

There are a few different types of entrapment:

- hair entrapment;
- limb entrapment;
- body entrapment;
- evisceration/disembowelment; and
- mechanical entrapment.

Drain covers must be installed over all suction outlets to prevent entrapment. The screws of the covers may be of a different color to distinguish them for inspection purposes.

The Virginia Graeme Baker Pool and Spa Safety Act was enacted by the U.S. Congress and signed into law on December 19, 2007. Designed to prevent the tragic and hidden hazard of drain entrapments and eviscerations in pools and spas, the law became effective on December 19, 2008. Under the law, all public pools and spas must have ASME/ANSI A112.19.8-2007-compliant drain covers installed, with a second anti-entrapment system installed when there is a single main drain other than an unblockable drain.

All operating public pools and spas must have drain covers on every drain and grate that meet the ASME/ANSI A112.19.8–2007 standard.

If a pool has a single main drain (other than an unblockable drain), or multiple drains less than 3 feet apart, the operator must either disable the drain(s) or install a second anti-entrapment device or system. This can take the form of an automatic pump shut-off system, a gravity drainage system, a safety vacuum-release system (SVRS), or a suction-limiting vent system.

Mandatory federal requirements for entrapment avoidance, according to the Virginia Graeme Baker Pool and Spa Safety Act, require:

safety drain covers: Each swimming pool or spa drain cover manufactured, distributed or entered into commerce in the United States shall conform to the American National Standard ASME A112.19.8: "2007 Suction Fittings for Use in Swimming Pools, Wading Pools, Spas and Hot Tubs," published by the American Society of Mechanical Engineers (ASME). Compliance with this Standard will be enforced by the Consumer Product Safety Commission (CPSC) as a consumer product-safety rule;

public pool drain covers: Each public pool and spa (as defined), both new and existing, shall be equipped with drain covers conforming to the ASME/ANSI A112.19.8 2007 Standard described above; and

public pool drain systems: Each public pool and spa (pump) with a single main drain, other than an unblockable drain, shall be equipped with one or more additional devices or systems designed to prevent suction entrapment that meet the requirements of any applicable ASME/ANSI Standard or applicable consumer product-safety rule. In addition to a compliant drain cover, such additional devices or systems must include a safety vacuum-release system (SVRS), or suction-limiting vent system, or gravity drainage system, or automatic pump shut-off system, or drain disablement, or other system determined by the CPSC to be equally effective in preventing suction entrapment.

As of December 20, 2008, all drain covers for public pools and spas are required to comply with these rules. Anti-entrapment covers are designed to keep torsos and arms from blocking the cover, and they'll prevent hair from getting entangled.

Dual main drains installed far enough apart can also prevent entrapment. Removing main drains and installing gutter systems can help prevent entrapment.

Quiz 3

1. To understand how a pool or spa works, you can follow the path that the _____ takes in a pool or spa system.

☐ electricity

☐ chlorine

☐ water

2. T/F: Main drains are usually located at the shallowest part of a pool.

☐ True

☐ False

3. T/F: The main drain should be visually inspected regularly (ideally, daily), particularly when the pool is being serviced or when the pool floor is being swept.

☐ True

☐ False

4. The highest concentration of contamination is located at the _____ of the pool.

☐ bottom

☐ surface

☐ walls

5. Most skimmers have _____, which are the small floating, hinged devices that allow water to enter the skimmer.

☐ anchors

☐ gates

☐ lips

☐ weirs

6. T/F: The Virginia Graeme Baker Pool and Spa Safety Act was designed to prevent the tragic and hidden hazard of drain entrapments and eviscerations in pools and spas.

☐ True

☐ False

Answer Key is on page 83.

Section 5: Pipes

The pump is the heart of the circulation system, and the pipes are the veins and arteries.

There are many different types of plumbing you might see at a pool or spa, including galvanized steel, copper, ABS and PVC plastic. You will find most of the visible plumbing for the pool near the equipment (possibly, in a mechanical room). Outside of the equipment room, most (if not all) of the plumbing will be buried, making an inspection impossible.

PVC piping and fittings are commonly used for residential swimming pools. PVC pipes are non-toxic and are able to withstand pressure. The best choice for this use is Schedule 40 PVC. You will be looking for a white pipe that has identification printed on the side of the pipe itself. Black ABS with glued fittings, and old, black poly pipe with clamped fittings comply with the old industry standards. They are no longer considered ideal for swimming pool installations.

Any forms of metal, brass or copper pipes may be considered unacceptable in your jurisdiction. It's just a matter of time before a major leak or failure occurs with that type of pool plumbing system.

Metal pipes, including copper plumbing, are quickly disappearing from pool and spa installation practices. Metal rusts and corrodes, especially with caustic pool water and spa chemicals moving through the pipes.

The stronger the plastic pipe is, the higher its schedule number. The schedule number is always identified on the pipe itself. Schedule 40 PVC pipe is commonly used for pool plumbing. Some gas lines are plumbed with Schedule 80 PVC. It is designed to carry unheated water of below 100° F. CPVC, PEX and PB plastic pipe are often identified as rated for 180° F at 100 psi (82° C at 690 kPa). These pipes can actually withstand temperatures in excess of 212° F (100° C).

Piping that is exposed to freezing conditions should have a slope in one direction and a provision for draining. Alternatively, the piping system should have some other way to remove the water to prevent damage from freezing.

PVC pipe can be deteriorated by sunlight and UV radiation. Over time, PVC exposed to the sun loses its structural integrity and becomes brittle. There are PVC pipes that have been designed for sunlight exposure. The best practice is to not have any pipe directly exposed to sunlight. A preventative measure is to simply paint any pipe that is exposed to sunlight.

Support

If you find some pipes that need support—for example, pipes that might be running above the ground and under a deck—then the pipes will require support every 6 to 8 feet. Remember that 2-inch pipes filled with water are extremely heavy and require adequate support. Not only are the pipes heavy, but they are being vibrated by the flow of water and the pump action. Look for any sagging or unsupported pipes.

Rubber Fittings

You may find connections of pipe using rubber fittings with stainless steel straps or clamps. These fittings indicate that glue was not used. There may have been a repair at this location, or it's possible that there wasn't a lot of room to work to install the pipes properly, or there may be other reasons. The problem is that these rubber fittings or connections can break, leak, wear out or fail when under a lot of pressure.

Size

Typically, the plumbing was installed according to local plumbing codes. The equipment for pools and spas is usually plumbed together already. The plumbing is commonly 1½- or 2-inch pipe. The pump is commonly designed for a 1½-inch pipe. If you do see exposed piping, the larger the pipes, the better, because when the pipe is large, there is less restriction in the flow of water and, therefore, less strain on the equipment. A reduction in size of the plumbing pipe is not allowed.

Return Inlets

Once the water is filtered and heated, it must be returned to the pool or spa through the return inlets. Return inlets are sometimes called return fittings, inlet ports, or discharge outlets. Return ports are part of the process of directing the water flow for good circulation throughout the pool. Good flow through the pool provides equal distribution of chemicals and heated water throughout the entire pool. Good flow patterns also eliminate dead or stagnant areas.

Wall inlets are usually shaped like eyeballs that rotate, and are adjustable.

Water Levels

Checking the water level is part of the inspection. The water level in a pool can go down by evaporation. There are generally three ways to fill the pool when the water level is down. One way is to use a garden hose and stand there for a couple of hours filling the pool, which is obviously impractical. Another way is to use a mechanical timer with a valve. The valve can be set to open up and run water to fill the pool for a timed interval, which can be anywhere from one to 60 minutes. These valves are reliable, but they tend to stick. There are valves that are calibrated not by time but by gallons. One of the best types of valve is a float valve. It operates the same way as the float inside a toilet tank (water closet). When the water level drops, the float senses it. The float could be installed in a skimmer unit, or it could be at a separate tank or reservoir. Keeping the pool and spa filled with water helps prevent the buildup of calcium on the tiles.

Quiz 4

1. The _____ is the heart of the circulation system, and the pipes are the veins and arteries.

    ☐ filter

    ☐ heater

    ☐ pool

    ☐ pump

2. _____ piping and fittings are commonly used for residential swimming pools.

    ☐ ABS

    ☐ Copper

    ☐ PEX

    ☐ PVC

3. Schedule _____ PVC pipe is commonly used for pool plumbing.

    ☐ 10

    ☐ 20

    ☐ 40

    ☐ 80

4. Once the water is filtered and heated, it must be returned to the pool or spa through the _____.

    ☐ output holes

    ☐ return inlets

    ☐ skimmer ports

    ☐ water spouts

Answer Key is on page 84.

Section 6: Valves

Valves control the flow of the water in a pool or spa. There are several common types of valves, including:

- gate valves;
- ball valves;
- butterfly or water valves;
- multi-port (3-port) valves;
- globe valves; and
- check valves.

3-Port Valves

Manual 3-port valves function following the shape of the letter Y, where the flow of water can come up from the stem and be controlled and diverted to either or both branches. A 3-port valve can also gather water from the two branches above, combine the water, and direct it to the stem below. The diverter of the valve controls which direction the water flows and how much water going one way is combined with the water going the other way. All 3-port valves function in basically the same way.

A typical 3-port valve is designed for 1½-inch or 2-inch pipes. It has a diverter. It has either a handle (for manual control) or a motor (for motorized control). These valves are commonly found if the pool and spa are connected to the same single pump, filter and heating system. If the 3-port valve is connected with a pool and spa, the water from the pool enters one end, the water from the spa enters the other, and the diverter determines how much water flows from each stem and controls the mixing of the two paths of water. This valve is handy to use when one of the containers (pool or spa) is being drained.

When the diverter is designed with a gasket, then it's referred to as a positive seal. A positive-seal valve allows water to flow in one direction without allowing any water to bypass its intended direction. When a diverter is designed without a gasket, then it's referred to as a non-positive seal valve, which acts more like a baffle that directs most of the water in the intended direction, and allows some bypass.

As with most pool and spa equipment, stainless steel fasteners and screws should be used.

Not too much can go wrong with a manual 3-port valve. Smooth operating requires regular lubrication. Lubrication is the most important maintenance item for any 3-port valve. A pure silicone lubricant should be used. Most other lubricants are petroleum-based, which should not be used as they will dissolve gaskets and cause leaks. Lubrication of the valves is recommended every six months.

Leaks can occur at a 3-port valve. The valve might leak at the cover, the shaft, at the pipe connections, or inside the valve itself. A common leak area is at the gasket. Replacement of the gasket is recommended.

At a motorized valve, look for a clean motor that has no signs of rust or corrosion. If there is a solar-panel heating system installed, warping may be found. If a solar panel is installed and heats water to greater than 200° F, which then backflows into the valves, the super-heated water may warp the components.

A motorized or automatic valve has a small motor installed in the same place that the handle would be located on a manual valve. Motorized valves are installed on the plumbing system for a few reasons, such as for valves that are located far away or are difficult to access.

Another reason to have motorized or automatic valves installed on the plumbing system of a pool is to create a reverse flow of water during the heating cycle. During normal operation, water is taken from the main drain and skimmer, heated, and then returned to the pool through ports located at about 18 to 24 inches below the water surface. The idea of having a reverse flow of water during the heating cycle is to have water drawn from those previously mentioned shallow ports (18 to 24 inches below the water), heated, and then pushed to the main drain in the floor of the pool. The purpose here is to have the heated water rise up through the pool, just like hot air rising upward through cooler air. The heated water warms the pool uniformly. In a normal heating cycle, only the top few feet of the pool water is cycled and heated. Either way works; some people like the reverse-flow concept, thinking that it has a few added benefits. Both methods require heating the water and cycling it through the system until the entire pool water reaches the desired temperature.

If the motor is found to be burned out, it is easy to replace, and it does not require total replacement of the valve—just the motor. Sometimes, a motor will move out of position because the screws or the mounting bracket holding the motor in place have become loose.

Shut-Off Valves

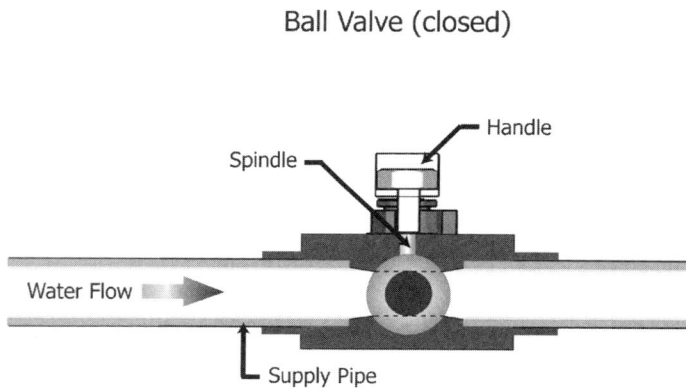

Ball Valve (closed)

Gate and ball valves are installed on the plumbing system for a pool or spa in order to stop (or shut off) the flow of water. On older systems, shut-off valves might be installed and used as a 3-port valve.

A ball valve is a valve with a sphere (or ball) inside it. The ball is the part that controls the flow through it. A ball valve can be totally open, totally closed, or any position in between. The ball has a hole through the middle so that when the port is in line with the pipe, water will flow. When the valve is closed, the hole is perpendicular, and the flow is stopped. The handle indicates if the ball is in line with the flow. When the handle is at a right-angle to the pipe, the valve is closed. Ball valves are very effective for shut-off applications.

Gate valves are meant to be fully open or closed. A gate valve permits you to completely stop, but not modulate, the flow within a pipe. It should not be used in a partially open or partially closed position. The gate valve has a handle that drives a worm screw-style shaft inside a threaded gate. Remember: "Righty-tighty, lefty-loosey."

Check Valves

The check valve allows water to flow in only one direction. A check valve might be installed to prevent hot water from flowing back into the filter. A check valve might be used to stop the flow of caustic chemicals of a chlorinator from flowing in the wrong direction. Check valves could be swing-gate valves or spring-loaded gate valves. Inside a flapper check valve, the water is stopped by a flapper that moves (opens or closes), according to the flow of water. Inside a spring-loaded gate valve, the water pressure pushes on the spring-loaded gate.

All check valves can become clogged with debris. Check valves might remain open if clogged. A 90-degree check valve is one that has an access port to open and clean or replace the valve's interior. Some check valves are made of clear PVC that allows you to check the operation and water flow.

Unions

Union fittings are very handy when the need to repair or replace exists, and cutting and reconnecting plumbing are necessitated. When a piece of equipment needs to be disconnected from the system and removed, and there are union fittings installed, the task becomes easier. Unions allow a contractor to remove and replace equipment without installing new plumbing.

Quiz 5

1. Manual 3-port valves function following the shape of the letter ___, where the flow of water can come up from the stem and be controlled and diverted to either or both branches.

    ☐ S

    ☐ V

    ☐ X

    ☐ Y

2. T/F: Three-port valves are typically found if the pool and spa are connected to the same single pump, filter and heating system.

    ☐ True

    ☐ False

3. A _____ valve can be totally open, totally closed, or any position in between.

    ☐ ball

    ☐ gate

    ☐ float

    ☐ 3-port

4. A _____ valve permits you to completely stop, but not modulate, the flow within a pipe, and should not be used in a partially open or partially closed position.

    ☐ ball

    ☐ gate

    ☐ float

    ☐ 3-port

5. _____ allow a contractor to remove and replace equipment without installing new plumbing.

    ☐ Locks

    ☐ Plug and cord lines

    ☐ Unions

    ☐ Valves

Answer Key is on page 84.

Section 7: Solar Heating Systems

There are many manufacturers, styles and types of solar heating systems, including panels and controls. Some are plastic, metal, thin aluminum, rubber, and indirect coil. Some are very basic, and some are highly complex and costly. Some modern solar panels have sensors that track the movement of the sun and move on more than one axis. No matter how complex, the plumbing is generally similar to that of a pool or spa. Look for leaks. If the panels are located on the roof, be very careful and protect yourself with safety practices.

Basically, solar panels are designed to absorb heat from the sun and transfer that heat-energy to the liquid passing through the panels. The concept is to have the water heated by the solar panels before going to the pool's heater. The sun is used first before any fossil fuels.

Types of Solar Heating Systems

The most common type of solar heating system is an open-loop system. It is "open" to the pool water. The pool water circulates through the panels.

A closed-loop solar heating system is one that is separate from the pool water. The liquid flowing through the panels is heated and sent to a heat exchanger in which the pool water is circulated. The heated solar-panel water inside the exchanger transfers its heat to the pool water circulating outside the exchanger. The heat exchanger is typically a coil. Closed systems are used in cold-in-winter climates and in desert climates, where it is hot by day and cold by night, whereas water in an open system might freeze, then expand and crack the panels. In a closed system, the harsh chemicals in the pool water do not circulate through the sensitive solar panels.

A solar-panel heating system is installed in between the filter and the pool's heating equipment. The purpose is to filter the water before it travels to the solar heating system, and also to heat the water with the sun before using fossil fuels.

A thermostat is installed with the solar panel heater. It senses the temperature of the water in the solar panel system and compares it to the temperature of the water coming out of the filter. If the water coming out of the filter is lower in temperature than that which can be heated in the solar panel, then a motorized valve is activated, and water is directed to the panels to heat the pool water. The valve is called an automatic bypass valve (a 3-port motorized valve).

The main component to look for is the 3-port valve. That valve controls the direction of the water that comes from the filter. The valve directs the water to either the heating system or equipment, or it sends it to the solar panels. There's also a check valve installed (which may also be a 3-port valve) on the line coming from the solar panels.

This check valve prevents water from entering the solar panel system when the solar panels are not being used.

Determining how many solar panels are required in relation to the size of the pool or spa is important but may not be necessary to your inspection. Most inspectors will "eye it up," so to speak, with some general measurements and rules of thumb. The general rule of thumb for determining the size of solar panels required in relation to the size of the pool or spa is that around 70% of the surface area of the pool and spa should be the same as the surface area of the solar panels, like this:

60% to 75% of the surface area of the pool and spa =
the surface area of the solar panels.

Solar panels should face the sun, so they are generally installed facing south. Winds may have to be factored in when checking the location of solar panels. Prevailing winds may cool the panels so much that they won't be effective.

It's a good idea to make sure that all of the pipes and lines going to and coming from the panels are insulated. The insulation prevents heat from escaping the system.

The solar panels should be inspected for leaks every month. Leaks may be caused by the expansion and contraction of different materials of the solar panel system. One common maintenance issue is the debris and dirt that collect on the panels. Dirty panels are inefficient. They can be easily cleaned with some soap and water. Check for dirty panels.

Another thing to keep in mind is poor circulation through the panels. If possible, ask the property owner about the performance of the solar-panel heating system. If there's a problem with the solar panels, it could come from scale and buildup inside the panels. The hard pool water and chemicals may cause clogging with scale inside the panels. The scale can be cleaned, but this requires taking the panels apart.

Common Problems to Check for with Solar Panels

If a panel is leaking water, the water chemistry should be checked, as hard or caustic water can create problems. Also, connections might be loose.

If the water is not warming up enough, it might be because:

- the panels are too small;
- the panels are improperly oriented;
- the controls are not working properly; and/or
- the water is circulating through the panels at the wrong time of day.

If there are air bubbles in the solar panel system during operating times, then check to see if the filter is dirty, or whether the vacuum-relief valve has stopped working.

Quiz 6

1. T/F: The best idea is to have the water heated by the pool heater before going to the solar panels.

    ☐ True

    ☐ False

2. The most common type of solar heating system is a(n) _____-loop system.

    ☐ closed

    ☐ open

3. T/F: A common maintenance issue is debris and dirt collecting on the panels.

    ☐ True

    ☐ False

4. A(n) _____-loop solar heating system is one that is separate from the pool water.

    ☐ closed

    ☐ open

Answer Key is on page 84.

Section 8: Pumps and Motors

The pool pump is the heart of the system. The pump is what moves the water. The motor is what turns electricity into mechanical energy. Swimming pool pumps are centrifugal pumps. A centrifugal pump has an impeller that rotates on an axis, creating a centrifugal force and displacement of the water. As the pump's internal component spins, it shoots water out of it at a high velocity.

While spinning, a vacuum is created that sucks more water toward the pump. Pool pumps are self-priming. When a pool pump starts, it pushes out the air in the system first. A vacuum is then created, which sucks water into the system. The pump pushes the water that passes throughout the plumbing system.

All pool pumps have similar parts, including:

- a volute;
- an impeller;
- mechanical seals;
- a motor adaptor and seal plate; and
- the shaft.

The volute is sometimes called the diffuser. It gives a self-priming pump the ability to handle the air and re-prime itself. It contains the impeller. It is the pressure chamber in which the impeller is spinning.

The impeller moves the water by spinning. The impeller is located inside the volute, spinning and creating suction. The volute is the device from which the water is forced out of the pump and into the plumbing system. When the impeller spins, it forces water out of the pump and, at the same time, it creates a vacuum in the strainer pot that sucks water into the pump.

Attached to the pump is the strainer pot. The strainer pot filters out and traps small debris, such as hair. The strainer pot at the pump is similar to the skimmer at the surface area of the pool or spa. The skimmer is designed to catch and filter out large debris, such as leaves. The strainer pot needs to be cleaned and maintained. It should be routinely pulled out and cleaned. If the pot is not clean, then the water flow will be restricted. If the water doesn't flow adequately, then it won't be filtered adequately, and the water will be cloudy.

The strainer is typically bolted or otherwise attached to the volute. The volute is part of the pump. In spas where debris is not a problem, there probably is no strainer pot installed. The strainer pot attached to the pump likely has an O-ring in between. Check there for a water leak. If the O-ring fails, the pump will suck air into the system through the deteriorated ring. On the bottom of the strainer is a plug that can be used for draining and winterization.

Cavitation is a symptom of a problem. It can occur when the impeller doesn't have enough water. Cavitation can be created when the capacity of the motor to push out water exceeds the intake. Bubbling and vibration could be the result of cavitation. The sound of the pump changes when it is cavitating.

There are several reasons for cavitation occurring, including:

- the pump is oversized;
- there is debris in the skimmer;
- the filter is dirty;
- there is a restriction in the suction line; and/or
- there is a leak on the vacuum-side of the system.

The shaft is the cylinder coming out of the motor. It is the part that turns the impeller. When this turns, water is flowing. There is a seal around the spinning shaft. Check the seal. The seal allows the shaft to spin while preventing the pump from leaking water.

Motors are sized or rated by horsepower (hp). Typical sizes of motors for pools and spas range from ½-hp to 2 hp. It takes a considerable amount of energy to start a motor. The capacitor, which stores an electrical charge, gives the motor a jolt of electricity to start it. The capacitor is usually located on the top of the motor. The most common motor used for a pool is one that uses a capacitor. A typical motor is a 110/220-volt-type.

Nameplate

A nameplate should be attached to the motor. The nameplate has a lot of useful information on it that you may need to record for your inspection, including:

- manufacturer;
- manufacture date;
- amperage;
- horsepower; and
- duty.

In addition to the basic identifying information, the nameplate tells you the amperage. The first number is the start-up amperage draw. The second number is the normal running draw, in amps. The nameplate may show the duty rating, too.

Turnover Rate

The turnover rate of a pool refers to how long it takes for all of the water inside the pool to circulate once through the entire system, including the filter. Ideally, the entire pool capacity will cycle through the filter at least twice a day. But turnover rate requirements or recommendations vary for different types of water use. It depends on the type of pool (residential or commercial), the bather load, and the volume of water. Local codes may regulate the turnover rate. In most jurisdictions, the standards require a pool to cycle through once every six hours. Turnover rates for spas may be 30 minutes. Wading pool turnover rates may be one to two hours.

Inspection

The pump and motor are the heart of the system. It is very important to check the pump and motor. Keeping the pump in good, functional shape involves keeping it dry and cool. Use your eyes and ears. Use your eyes to check for leaks. A leak from a motor is a motor that needs repair. Use your ears to listen for problems with the motor during operation. A bad motor will tell you that it's bad by the way it sounds. A bad motor might also vibrate. A noisy motor will often have worn-out bearings. Sometimes, it's a bent shaft.

Tips

- The motor should be dry.
- The motor should be clean and free of debris.
- There should be no leaks.
- The strainer pot should be clean.
- The pump should not vibrate.
- There should be no unusual or unexpected noises.
- The pump should not be hot.

Motors should stay dry, but they often get very wet. Exposed motors get hit with weather and rain. Motors sometimes get wet when splashed during maintenance. Sometimes, the process of cleaning the filter gets the motor wet. Look for rust and corrosion at the motor and pump.

Quiz 7

1. The _____ is what moves the water, and the _____ is what turns electricity into mechanical energy.

   ☐ pump..... motor

   ☐ motor..... pump

2. The _____ moves the water by spinning.

   ☐ impeller

   ☐ pot

   ☐ shaft

   ☐ volute

3. Attached to the pump is the _____, which filters out and traps small debris, such as hair.

   ☐ cartridge port

   ☐ DE filter

   ☐ skimmer

   ☐ strainer pot

4. _____ is a symptom of a problem which can occur when the impeller doesn't have enough water.

   ☐ Air dispersion

   ☐ Blockage

   ☐ Cavitation

5. The _____ rate of a pool refers to how long it takes for all of the water inside the pool to circulate once through the entire system, including the filter.

   ☐ rollover

   ☐ turnover

   ☐ trickle

6. T/F: A bad pool motor will tell you that it's bad by the way it sounds.

   ☐ True

   ☐ False

Answer Key is on page 84.

Section 9: Electrical

Because of the great potential of electrical shock hazards around a swimming pool and spa, this section of the training material covers the standards and requirements regarding the wiring in and around swimming pools and spas. The following information was adapted from:

- the International Residential Code (IRC) 2006 Codes, Chapter 41: Swimming Pools;
- the National Fire Protection Association, 2005 (NFPA 70-05); and
- the National Electrical Code®.

A conductive path for fault current can be easily made through the water to the earth. When a bather touches an energized metal component, the fault-current path through that bather could be fatal.

A swimmer floating in the pool, not touching anything but the surrounding water, could become part of a fault-current path, too. If an electrical device, such as a portable radio, falls into the swimming pool, an electrical potential might be created in the pool that could cause that person to be surrounded by different levels of voltage in the water, acting like a conductor.

Dry-Niche Luminaire

A dry-niche luminaire is installed behind a window below the water level and does not allow any water penetration. Typical residential installations have access through the deck box. The glass window is sealed and waterproof.

Forming Shells

The forming shell for the luminaire is built into the pool wall and supports the wet-niche luminaire.

No-Niche Luminaires

This is an underwater luminaire that is attached to the pool's wall surface. A mounting bracket is used. Typically, no-niche luminaires are installed in above-ground pools.

Underwater Luminaires

An underwater luminaire must be designed to assure freedom from electrical shock without a GFCI (ground-fault circuit interrupter) device in its circuit. Any light fixture operating at more than 15 volts must have GFCI protection. Portable luminaires must not have any exposed metal parts.

Wet-Niche Luminaires

A wet-niche luminaire is intended for installation in

Underwater Lighting For Pools

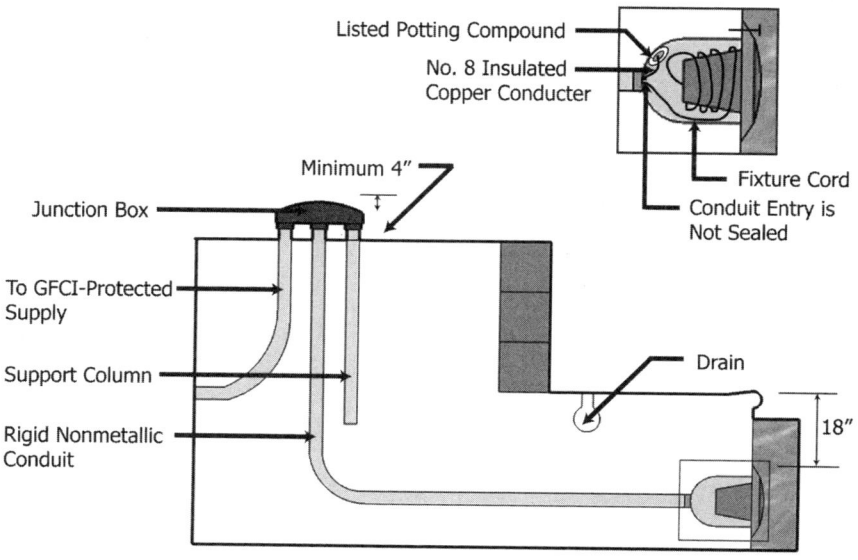

Listed Potting Compound

No. 8 Insulated Copper Conducter

Minimum 4"

Junction Box

To GFCI-Protected Supply

Support Column

Rigid Nonmetallic Conduit

Fixture Cord

Conduit Entry is Not Sealed

Drain

18"

a forming shell mounted in a pool wall. The forming shell is installed before the concrete is placed. The forming shell is not sealed from the pool water. The wet-niche luminaire fixture is designed to have water completely surrounding it. A wet-niche luminaire is connected with a permanently attached, flexible cord at least 12 feet long that extends to a junction box, typically at the pool deck. To re-lamp, it should have a coiled cord long enough to allow it to be pulled up out of the water without the cord becoming disconnected.

A wet-niche luminaire supplied by a flexible cord must have all exposed metal parts grounded by an insulated copper equipment grounding conductor. That conductor must be integral to the cord. And it must be connected to a grounding terminal in the supply junction box, transformer enclosure, or other enclosure, and must not be smaller than the supply conductors, and must be not be smaller than 16 AWG.

Luminaire Location

The top of the fixture lens of a luminaire must be at least 18 inches below the normal water level of a permanent pool, except where the luminaire is listed for use at other depths. For a portable pool, the luminaire can be between 8 to 10 inches below the top of the pool wall.

Flexible Cords

Flexible cords are used for easy removal of fixtures to repair or replace them. For other than underwater luminaires or fixed equipment rated at 20 amps or less, flexible cords can be used. For other than storable pools, the flexible cord cannot be longer than 3 feet. Cords that supply electricity to swimming pool equipment must have a copper-equipment grounding conductor not smaller than 12 AWG, and shall be provided with a grounding-type attachment plug.

Underwater fixtures, such as no-niche and wet-niche fixtures, can have cords longer than 3 feet so that the fixture can be removed and brought up to the deck for repair.

Some equipment for a storable pool could have longer cords, too, because it is not fixed or stationary.

The equipment grounding conductors should not be smaller than the supply conductors, and not smaller than 16 AWG.

A listed spa- or hot tub-assembly packaged unit installed outside can have a long cord-and-plug connection, but it has to have GFCI protection, and the cord cannot be longer than 15 feet. A listed spa- or hot tub-assembly packaged unit installed indoors can have a long cord-and-plug connection, but it has to be rated 20 amps or less.

Weatherproof Receptacle Cover

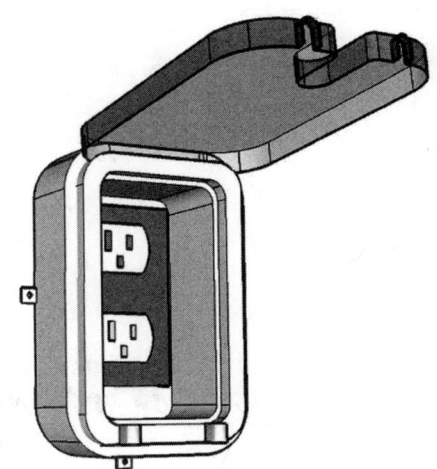

Receptacles

When measuring clearances between a pool or spa and a receptacle, measure the distance as the shortest path that an appliance supply cord connected to the receptacle would follow without penetrating a floor, wall, ceiling, doorway, window, or other effective, permanent barrier.

Only receptacles for specific equipment are permitted between 6 and 10 feet from the inside wall of the pool. They must be a single receptacle of the locking and grounding type, so that a typical radio, for example, could not be plugged into it. The receptacle must also be GFCI-protected. There must not be any receptacles that supply power to appliances within 10 feet of the inside wall of the pool or spa. All other receptacles must not be located within 6 feet of the inside walls of the pool, spa or hot tub.

At least one 125-volt, 15- or 20-ampere receptacle is required to be installed. It should be located at least 6 feet (and not farther than 20 feet) from the inside wall of the pool or outdoor spa or hot tub. This required receptacle should not be higher than 6½ feet from the floor, platform or ground at the pool or spa.

GFCI Protection Required

All 125-volt receptacles that are rated 30-ampere or less and located within 20 feet of the inside walls of the pool or outdoor spa or hot tub shall be protected by a GFCI. This is for portable and permanent pools and spas, indoor and outdoor. Receptacles that supply electricity to pumps and motors rated at 120 to 240 volts by receptacle or direct connection shall provide GFCI protection, regardless of their location.

Ground Fault Receptacle Protecting Entire Branch Circuit

LINE WIRES

LOAD WIRES

**DISTRIBUTION PANEL
(fuses or circuit breakers)**

black (HOT)
white (neutral)
bare or green (ground)

For portable pools, all electrical equipment, including power cords, shall be protected by GFCIs.

Ground-fault circuit-interrupting breakers protect circuits and people from ground faults. If a GFCI breaker is installed on a circuit, it will provide protection to all of the receptacles in that branch circuit downstream of the GFCI. The GFCI opens or breaks the circuit when it detects a ground fault. It does that by measuring the difference between the electrical current coming into it and the current going out of it.

GFCI breakers have trip and reset buttons to test that they are working properly. The inspector should test (or trip) the breaker using the test button to ensure that the GFCI is functioning and the circuit has been turned off.

There are three types of GFCIs that you may encounter in a pool and spa inspection. One is at the circuit breaker panelboard, where the GFCI looks like a standard circuit breaker.

The second type of GFCI is a GFCI receptacle, which looks similar to a standard electrical receptacle but has a test and reset button on it.

The third type of GFCI you might find is one that is portable, such as a GFCI device that is part of an extension cord, or a small device that is plugged into a receptacle, making that receptacle function as a GFCI.

If a GFCI will not reset, then further investigation is necessary because an electrical safety hazard may exist. Water and electricity do not mix safely.

Spa and Hot Tub GFCI

The outlet that supplies a self-contained spa or hot tub assembly with a heater load of 50 amperes or less should be protected by a GFCI.

Receptacles for Indoor Spas and Hot Tubs

There should be no receptacles within 6 feet from the inside walls of an indoor spa or hot tub. At least one 125-volt receptacle should be located between 6 to 10 feet from the inside walls of the indoor spa or hot tub. This helps prevent the hazards of using an extension cord.

All 125-volt receptacles of 30 amperes or less located within 10 feet of the inside walls of an indoor spa or hot tub shall have GFCI protection.

Switches

There should be no switches (including timers or panelboards) within 5 feet horizontally from the inside walls of a pool, spa or hot tub, except where separated from the pool, spa or hot tub by a permanent barrier, fence or wall. This standard prevents bathers from reaching a device. Or, the switches must be listed for use within 5 feet.

Means of Disconnect

There should be a means provided to simultaneously disconnect all ungrounded conductors for all equipment, except for lighting. Such means should be readily accessible and within sight of the equipment, and must be at least 5 feet away from the inside walls of the pool, spa or hot tub.

Overhead Conductor Clearances

There should be at least 22½ feet of clearance in any direction to the water level, the edge of the water surface, and the base of a diving platform, or permanently anchored raft. There must be at least 14½ feet of clearance in any direction to the diving platform.

Service Drop Clearances

18' road
10' sidewalk
3' roof pitch 4 in 12 or greater
22'6" high and 10' away horizontally
swimming pool

Paddle Fans and Luminaires Overhead

For outdoor pools and spas, luminaires and paddle fans are not permitted in the area over the water, and extending 5 feet horizontally from the inside edge of the pool to a distance of 12 feet above the water level.

For indoor pools and spas, there are some exceptions to not having luminaires and paddle fans installed overhead. Luminaires and paddle fans can be installed at least 12 feet above the water level without GFCI protection. However, if GFCI protection is provided, enclosed luminaires and fans are permitted as close as 7½ feet above the water.

Underground Wiring

Underground wiring should not be installed within 5 feet from the inside walls of pools or spas, unless installed inside a corrosion-resistant conduit or raceway.

Bonding

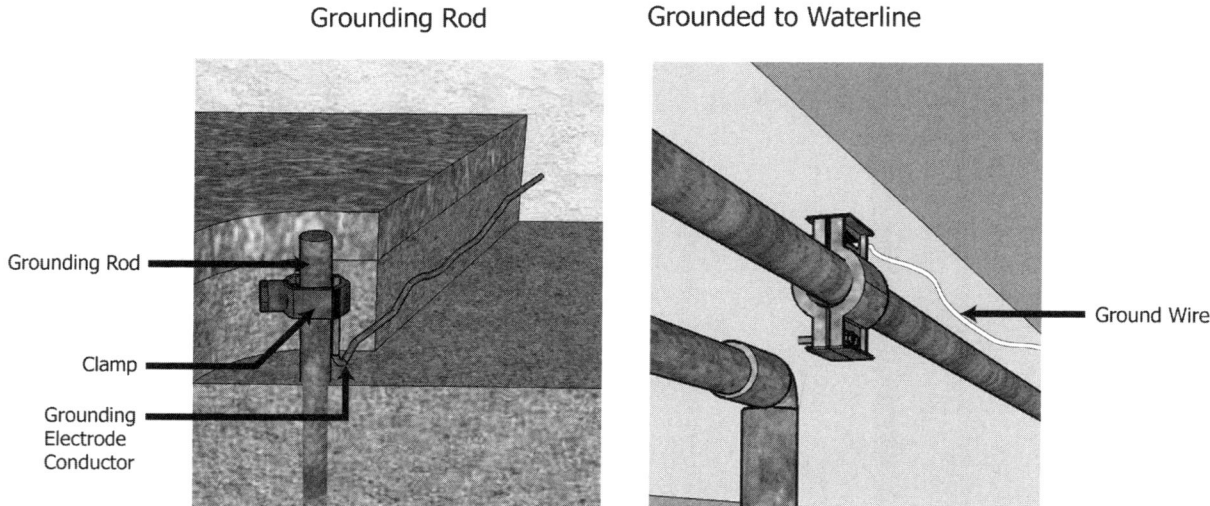

Grounding and bonding are required for different reasons. Bonding is required to get all metal parts of the electrical equipment and the non-electrical metal parts of the pool/spa structure to attain equal electrical potential. Bonding of metal parts of the electrical equipment makes a low-impedance path for fault current back to the source circuit to trip the over-current device. For equipment grounding, a separate, insulated copper grounding conductor should be run to the equipment-grounding terminal in the main service panel. Sheet metal screws must not be used to connect bonding conductors.

The following components of pools, spas and hot tubs must be bonded together using conductors of at least 8 AWG or using rigid metal conduit, including:

- conductive pool shells, including poured concrete, sprayed concrete, and concrete block with painted or plastered coatings;
- structural reinforcing steel;
- copper conductor grid;
- perimeter surfaces that extend 3 feet horizontally beyond the inside walls of the pool, spa or hot tub. A perimeter surface that extends less than 3 feet and is separated from the pool by a barrier shall require equipotential bonding on the pool-side of the barrier. Bonding to perimeter surfaces shall be provided and be attached to the pool, spa or hot tub reinforcing steel or copper conductor grid at a minimum of four points around the pool, spa or hot tub. There are some exceptions;
- metallic components;
- underwater lighting;

- metal fittings;
- electrical equipment; and
- all fixed metal parts.

Bonding is joining metallic parts to form an electrically conductive path that will result in electrical continuity between components to ensure that the electrical potential will be the same throughout. This is referred to as "equipotential bonding." Keeping the electrical potential at the same level reduces the hazard created by stray currents in the pool or in the ground around the pool. Connecting (or bonding) everything metallic in and around the pool will help eliminate voltage gradients (or differences in electrical potential) from one part of the pool to another, and from metallic equipment to the pool water.

The following is a general list of the items that require equipotential bonding:

- all metallic parts of the pool and spa;
- reinforcement metal of the pool, spa, coping, shell, framing, etc.;
- shells and mounting brackets of no-niche luminaires;
- all metal fittings;
- metal parts of the equipment;
- electrical devices and controls;
- metal cables and raceways, metal piping, and all metal parts; and
- water heaters rated at more than 50 amperes.

The bonding conductor should be at least 8 AWG or larger solid copper.

Grounding

The following equipment and components should be grounded:

- through-wall light assemblies and underwater luminaires, except for low-voltage;
- all electrical equipment within 5 feet of the inside wall of the pool, spa or hot tub;
- all electrical equipment associated with the filtering, heating and circulation;
- junction boxes;
- transformer and power supply enclosures;
- GFCIs; and
- panelboards that supply any electrical equipment of the pool, spa or hot tub.

Luminaires and related equipment should be grounded. All lighting assemblies and luminaires must be connected to an insulated copper equipment grounding conductor not smaller than 12 AWG.

Where a non-metallic conduit is installed, an 8 AWG insulated copper bonding jumper may be required to be installed in the conduit.

Wet-niche luminaires supplied by a flexible cord must have all exposed non-current-carrying metal parts grounded.

Pool motors must be grounded.

An equipment grounding conductor should be installed with the feeder conductors between the grounding terminal of the pool equipment panelboard and the grounding terminal of the applicable service equipment.

Pool Water Bonding

Where none of the bonded parts is making connection with the pool water, the pool water must be in direct contact with a conductive surface that exposes at least 9 square inches of surface area to the pool water at all times.

Panelboards

If there is a separate panelboard supplying the swimming pool equipment and it is fed from the service equipment, it must have an insulated equipment grounding conductor of at least 12 AWG run with the feeders from the service equipment.

Permanently Installed Radiant Heaters

Electric radiant heaters should not be installed over a pool or within 5 feet horizontally from the inside walls of the pool, and should be at least 12 vertical feet away from the pool deck.

Quiz 8

1. T/F: A swimmer floating in the pool, not touching anything but the surrounding water, could become part of a fault-current path.

    ☐ True

    ☐ False

2. A _____-niche luminaire is installed behind a window below the water level and does not allow any water penetration.

    ☐ wet

    ☐ dry

    ☐ no

    ☐ top

3. The _____-niche luminaire fixture is designed to have water completely surrounding it.

    ☐ wet

    ☐ dry

    ☐ no

    ☐ top

4. All 15- and 20-ampere, single-phase, 125-volt receptacles located within 20 feet of the inside walls of the pool and spa shall be protected by a(n) _____.

    ☐ AFCI

    ☐ GFCI

5. T/F: There should be no switches (including timers or panelboards) within 5 feet horizontally from the inside walls of pools, spas or hot tubs, except where separated by a barrier.

    ☐ True

    ☐ False

6. _____ bonding is joining metallic parts to form an electrically conductive path that will result in electrical continuity between components to ensure that the electrical potential will be the same throughout.

    ☐ Alternative

    ☐ Conductive

    ☐ Equipotential

    ☐ Major

7. The bonding conductor should be at least ___ AWG or larger solid copper.

☐ 2/0

☐ 4/0

☐ 6

☐ 8

Answer Key is on page 85.

Section 10: Filtration

Filtration and circulation are the means to provide clean, clear water. Filtration removes contaminants.

There are various types and styles of pool water filters. Some filters are made with tanks in which the water passing through is under pressure. Some tanks are not pressurized. There are three general types of filters you might find at a pool or spa:

- sand and gravel;
- DE; and
- cartridge.

Sand and Gravel Filters

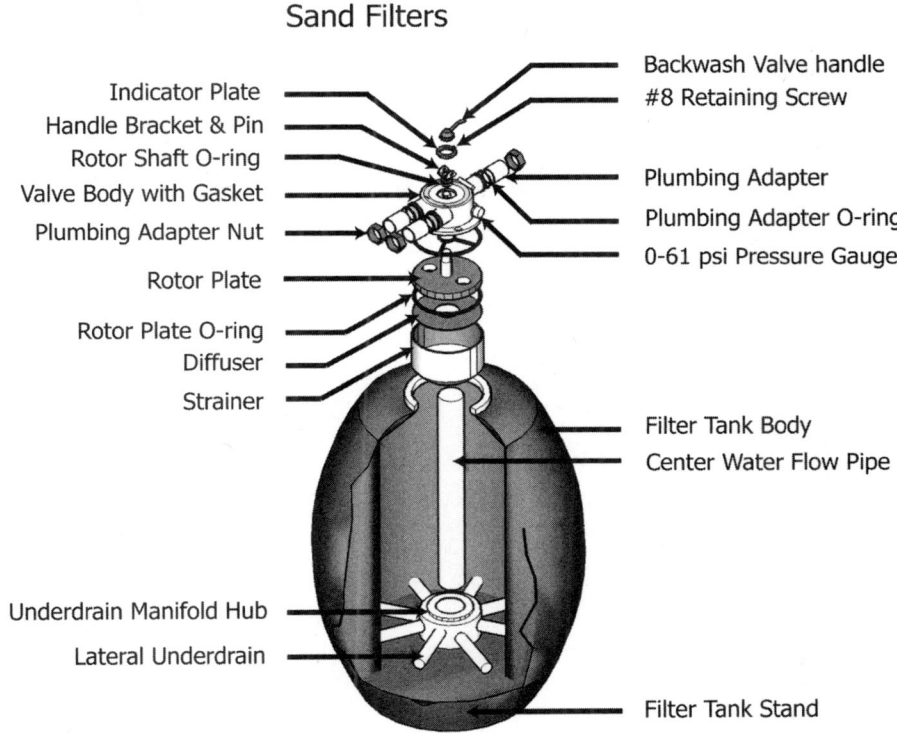

Sand Filters

Sand filters are the oldest type of pool filtration systems. At a sand and gravel filter, water enters a tank in which the sand and gravel material is located. Pressure can be created by pushing the water through the filtering medium. The impurities are filtered by the microscopic shapes of the sand and gravel. Some contractors add aluminum sulfate to the sand in order to improve efficiency.

There are sand and gravel filters that are free-flow, meaning that the water inside the filter tank is not under pressure. Free-flow sand and gravel filters are used mostly for decorative pools, such as fish ponds.

Sand filters are the least efficient, filtering particles down to about 60 microns. Cartridge filters go down to about 20 microns, making them better. There are DE filters that can filter particles down to about 8 microns, making these the best.

Sand filters need routine cleaning using the method of backwashing.

During your inspection, check the lids or covers of the filter tanks. Lids on filter tanks might leak. The lid might leak at the O-ring at the lid connection to the tank, or the leak might be at the relief-valve assembly on top of the tank lid.

Diatomaceous Earth (DE) Filters

Diatomaceous Earth Filter (Exploded View)

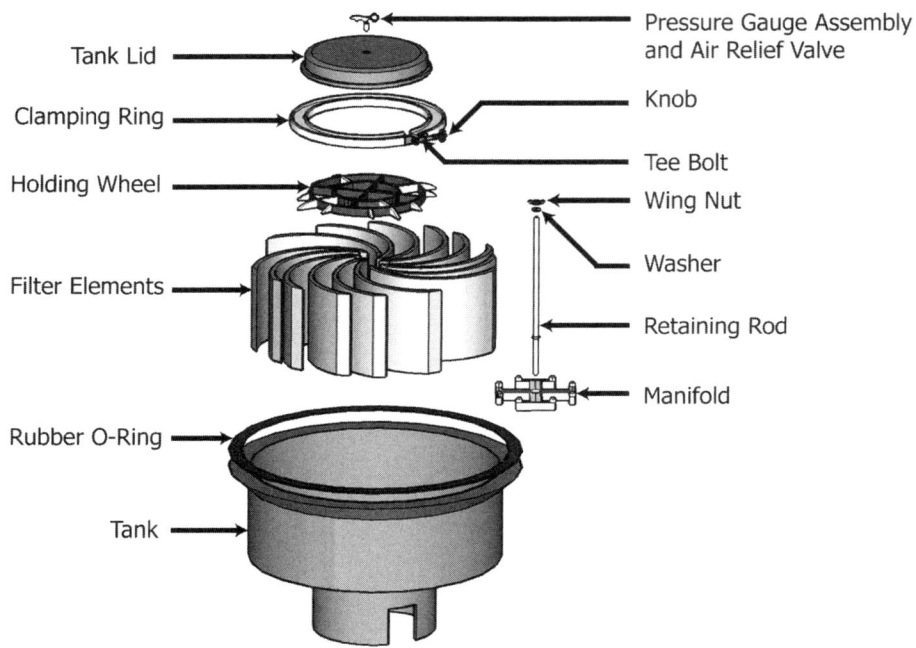

A diatomaceous earth filter is often called a DE filter. A DE filter is a disposable type of filter. At a DE filter, water enters a tank in which the filter is located. Water is under pressure inside the tank. The water passes through several grids. The grids are coated with a white, powder-like material. That material is the diatomaceous earth.

DE is actually finely crushed skeletons of microscopic organisms that lived on the earth millions of years ago. The DE is the medium that filters the water by absorbing impure particles, just like a sponge. The grids to which the DE is attached help keep the material from slumping into one large blob of material that would be ineffective for filtering.

When the DE filter is cleaned by backwashing, the powder is filtered out of the backwash by the use of a strainer bag in another tank that is located right next to the DE filter tank.

Cartridge

Cartridge filtration is a newer type of filtering system used for pools, but mostly for spas. Cartridge filters are ones in which pool water passes through cartridges of fine-mesh, pleated fabric. The fabric is the medium that filters the impurities from the water. A filter cartridge can be of a cylindrical, pleated arrangement. Cartridge filters are relatively small in size. They are replaceable. Cartridge filters are classified by square footage of filter surface (just as DE and sand filters are). Since the cartridge filter is pleated, a lot of square footage can be contained in a small area.

Cartridge filters are not backwashed but are removed from the filter, hosed off and cleaned.

Pressure Gauge

Most filter tanks have pressure gauges installed on the tank—typically, on the top of the tank. Sometimes, the gauge is installed on the multi-port valve. The gauge will read from 0 to 60 psi. Some jurisdictions require more than one pressure gauge to be installed on the water lines in order to measure the pressure differences before and after the filter tank. If the pressure before the filter is significantly greater than the pressure after the filter, this might indicate a dirty filter that needs cleaning.

Air Relief

On top of the tank, you may find an air-release valve. The purpose of the valve is to release air that has been trapped inside the tank.

T-Fitting

On top of the tank, you might find a T-fitting, which is a device shaped like a T. It holds an air-relief valve and a pressure gauge and secures those devices on top of the filter tank lid.

Backwash Valve

Backwashing is the way to clean the pool filter. Backwashing works on sand and DE filters, but not on cartridge filters. Cartridge filters do not require backwashing. Backwashing is a method by which water is pushed backwards through the filter, flushing out the dirt. A backwash valve is needed for this process. The valve can be a piston, rotary or multi-port valve. Rotary valves are used with DE filters. Multi-port valves are used with sand filters, and the use of a multi-port valve adds clean water to the pipes before the cycle of filtering begins again.

Backwash valves can leak. If the O-rings deteriorate, they might leak. If the valve leaks internally, then it might manifest as a drain of the water level in the pool. If the backwash is plumbed under the deck or hard-plumbed to a drain, the leak at the backwash valve may not be noticeable. Remember that a pool leak does not necessarily have to originate from the pool itself, but might come from a leak in the plumbing system or equipment somewhere.

Backwash Water

The backwash water is dirty and needs to be handled properly. The water can be hard-plumbed into the sewer line, or directed to a drain using a simple garden hose. If the chlorine level of the backwash water is low, the dirty water can be added to gardens and lawns. This is known as gray water.

Backwash Sight Glass

A sight glass comes in handy in order to keep an eye on the progress of the backwash. The sight glass can be installed on the discharge line. It's easier to use a sight glass to monitor the progress of the backwash than it is to watch the water at the far end of the hose.

Quiz 9

1. T/F: There are three general types of filters you might find at a pool or spa: sand and gravel; DE; and cartridge.

☐ True

☐ False

2. T/F: Of all the filter types, sand filters are the most efficient.

☐ True

☐ False

3. _____ filters are ones in which pool water passes through cartridges of fine-mesh, pleated fabric.

☐ Cartridge

☐ DE

☐ Gravel

☐ Sand

4. _____ is a way to clean a sand pool filter.

☐ Point-and-shoot washing

☐ Reverse-timing

☐ Front-washing

☐ Backwashing

Answer Key is on page 85.

Section 11: Pool Heaters

There are many types (and manufacturers) of various pool heaters, but they basically all work the same way. At a gas-fired heater, the hot exhaust from the flames rises up through the coils inside the heater. Pool water passes through the coils and absorbs heat. Cooler pool water enters the heater, passes through the coil, and warmer water exits the heater.

Most pool heaters are fueled by either natural gas or propane. Electric heaters are usually used for spas because of the cost of operation, and the slow heating and recovery time.

Heat pumps can be used for pool heaters. Heat pumps, instead of using gas or the sun, use the principles of gas compression to extract heat from the air and transfer it to the pool water. Heat pumps are efficient, they last a long time, and they don't get as dirty as fuel-fired heaters.

Less common are oil-fired pool heaters. The components, operation and maintenance of the oil-fired heater are much the same as for the gas-fired heater.

When pool water enters the heater through one port, it might pass through a multi-loop or serpentine coil made of copper tubing. While swirling through the copper-tubing heat exchanger, heat is exchanged from the hot gases to the pool water. The gas burners are located at the bottom of a gas-fired heater. The coils are located at the top of the heater.

The heater unit has a high-temperature switch installed on the heat exchanger. This switch keeps the circuit closed while the temperature of the heater is below a certain temperature, typically, 120° F to 150° F.

Pool heaters need routine inspection and maintenance. The gas burners in particular need regular cleaning.

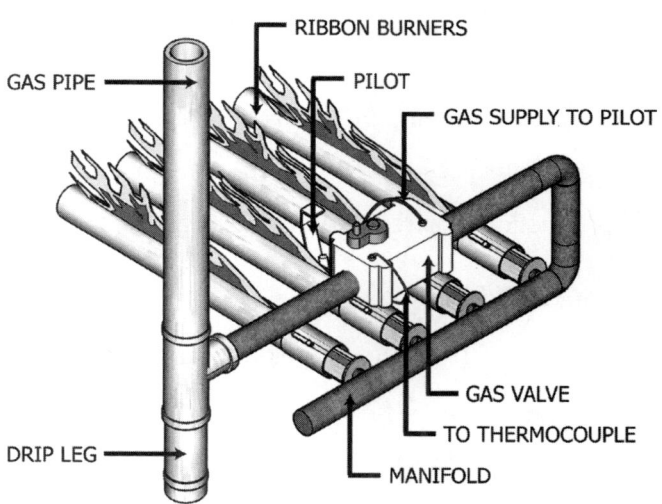

GAS SUPPLY TO BURNERS

Ignition Type

Gas heaters can be identified and described by the type of ignition system on the furnace. The different types of ignition systems are:

- standing pilot;
- intermittent-pilot or direct-spark; and
- hot-surface ignition.

The older gas furnaces have a standing pilot light that is always burning. Modern furnaces with higher efficiency ratings are slowly replacing these older, conventional gas furnaces.

Standing-Pilot

Standing-pilot gas heaters represent a significant number of pool heaters that are used today. A standing-pilot gas heater is equipped with a naturally aspirating gas burner, a draft hood, a solenoid-operated main gas valve, a continuously operating or standing-pilot light, a thermocouple safety device, a 24-volt AC transformer, and a heat exchanger.

The standing-pilot is the main distinguishing characteristic of the low-efficiency, conventional gas heater.

Mid-Efficiency

A mid-efficiency gas heater is equipped with a naturally aspirating gas burner and a pilot light. The pilot light is unlike a standing-pilot. It does not run continuously. The pilot light is shut off when the heater is not in operation (as when the thermostat is not calling for heat). There is no draft hood. There may be a small fan installed in the flue pipe to create an induced draft, so these heaters are sometimes referred to as induced-draft furnaces. Some mid-efficiency heaters have a motorized damper installed in the exhaust flue pipe. The intermittent pilot light is the main distinguishing characteristic.

High-Efficiency

High-efficiency gas heaters have annual fuel-utilization efficiency or AFUE ratings of 90% and greater. A solid-state control board controls the ignition. There is no continuous pilot light. Condensate is produced when heat is extracted from the flue gases. The temperature of the flue gases is low enough to use a PVC pipe as the vent exhaust pipe. There is no need to vent the exhaust gases up a chimney stack. There are two different types of high-efficiency furnaces:

• with an intermittent pilot or direct-spark; and

• with a hot-surface ignition system.

The production of excessive condensate is the main distinguishing characteristic.

Intermittent Pilot

INTERMITTENT PILOT LIGHT

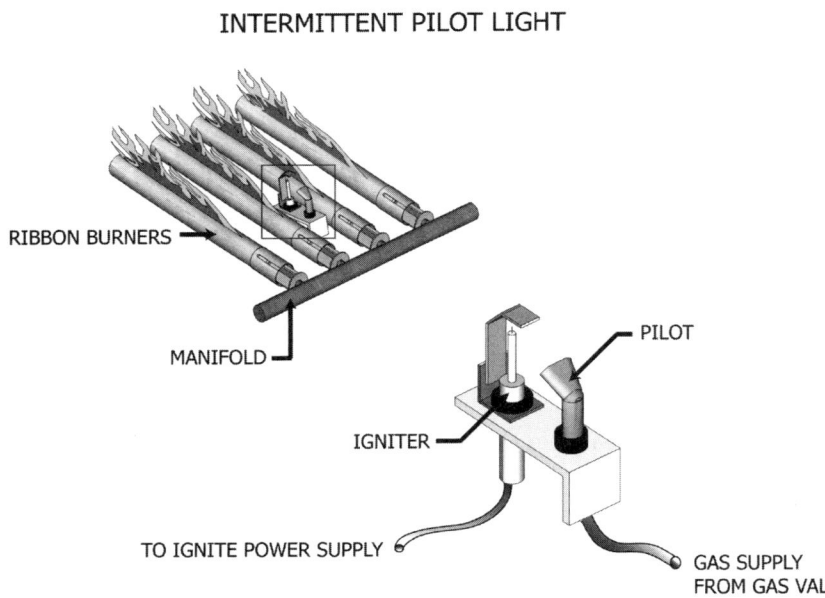

RIBBON BURNERS

MANIFOLD

IGNITER

TO IGNITE POWER SUPPLY

PILOT

GAS SUPPLY
FROM GAS VALVE

When the thermostat on a heater that has an intermittent pilot calls for heat, there is a short ignition period when a high-voltage spark is generated. The spark ignites the pilot.

If the pilot flame lights, the flame must be confirmed to be lit through a flame-confirmation process. If the flame is confirmed, a control module sends a signal to the main gas valve. The valve opens. The gas flows to the burner. The pilot flame lights the gas burner. The burners continue to burn until the thermostat is satisfied that it's at a desired temperature. The satisfied thermostat signals to stop the ignition process, and shuts off the pilot and burner.

Thermocouple

A thermocouple is a device that senses heat. A thermocouple is used in standing-pilot light gas heaters. It determines whether the pilot flame is lit before the main gas valve is opened to supply gas to the burners. The flame must be lit before the valve is opened.

The heat of the pilot flame is converted to electricity by the thermocouple. It turns heat into an electrical current. The current is strong enough to open the main gas valve. After being opened, the gas flows to the pilot light. If the thermocouple does not detect a pilot flame, it will turn off the gas supply to the pilot. The electrical current from a 24-volt AC transformer operates the main gas valve.

Thermopile

A thermopile is used in some standing-pilot gas furnaces instead of a thermocouple. A thermopile senses the heat from a pilot-light flame. It is larger than a thermocouple. It operates both the main gas valve and the pilot light. When there is a thermopile, there's no transformer required.

Mercury-Flame Sensor

A mercury-flame sensor might be used in an electronic ignition system. It consists of a sensor filled with mercury, a capillary tube, and a switch. The burner flame heats up the sensor.

Gas-Pressure Regulator

The pressure regulator is installed on the main gas valve. It regulates the gas pressure, ensuring a constant gas pressure in the burner manifold. For a propane-gas heating system, the regulator is located between the supply tank and the main gas valve.

Disconnects

There's usually a service-disconnect switch installed on the heating system. This switch turns off the electricity supplied to the heating system. It is typically a simple toggle switch.

The electricity supplied to the heating system should be on a separate, dedicated circuit that is not shared with wiring for any other purpose.

You may find that the wiring is installed so that the heating system will not turn on unless there is power being supplied to the pump and motor, too. The heater shouldn't turn on unless the pump and motor are also going to be circulating water.

Fireman's Switch

A "fireman's switch" is a simple on/off switch attached to a timer that shuts off the heater about 20 minutes before the pump.

Thermostats

There are basically two types of thermostats: mechanical and electronic. The mechanical thermostat has a dial that is set in between a blue and red color indicator on the dial. The mechanical thermostat is set using trial and error. An electronic thermostat uses an electronic sensor that sends signals to a control board.

Thermostats are set at the factory to prevent the water temperature from exceeding 105° F, but they can be adjusted to higher temperature limits.

Gas Valves

If the heater is gas-fired, there should be a separate gas shut-off valve installed just before the heater unit no farther than 6 feet from the unit. The valve should be installed upstream from the union fitting, connector, or quick-disconnect device it serves. Gas valves must be accessible.

A sediment trap is usually installed at the unit on the gas supply line, located downstream of the appliance shut-off valve, and as close to the appliance inlet as practical. This allows the sediment trap to be serviced (cleaned) after closing the upstream shut-off valve. The sediment trap should be installed at a change of direction in the gas flow to the appliance. Check your local code requirements.

Check for gas leaks. You can use some special equipment to detect gas leaks, or simply use your nose.

Vent Connections

Heating systems are commonly installed outside, but sometimes they are installed inside an equipment room. The vent for combustion gases should be installed according to the manufacturer's recommendations and the authority having jurisdiction (AHJ). If there is a chimney for the heater, connectors should be used to connect the heater to the vertical chimney or vent, except where the chimney or vent is attached directly to the appliance.

The vent connector should be as short as practical, and the appliance should be located as close as practical to the chimney or vent.

Flue Pipe

The flue is the passage through which the gases from the combustion chamber of the heater move to the outside. A flue is also referred to as the flue pipe, vent pipe, or vent connector. A chimney flue is the flue that is inside a chimney. The flue from the heating system to the chimney is often called the vent connector, chimney connector, or smoke pipe. A flue outlet, or vent, is the opening in a heating system through which the flue gases move.

Flue Details

The flue pipe (or vent pipe or vent connector) connects the outlet of the heater to the chimney. The flue pipe should not extend farther than the inner-liner surface of the chimney flue. Flue pipes from two appliances should not enter a chimney from opposite sides at the same height. From the point where a flue pipe enters the chimneystack, there should be at least 2 feet of clearance above the chimney cleanout.

There should be a slope of ¼-inch per linear foot of flue pipe. The flue pipe's horizontal run should not exceed 75% of the vertical run. The vent pipe crossovers in an attic should extend at an angle that is at least 60 degrees from the vertical.

The flue pipe should be at least the same diameter as the outlet of the furnace. The diameter of the flue pipe should never be reduced.

Draft Hood

A draft hood is installed on standing-pilot gas furnaces. Mid- and high-efficiency gas furnaces do not have draft hoods. A draft hood is attached to the top of the furnace above the flue outlet. It is sometimes called a draft diverter.

The draft hood's function is to produce a constant, low draft of air for the combustion chamber. It allows dilution air to be drawn into the vent pipe. The dilution air cools the exhaust and ensures a good draft. The draft hood also prevents large downdrafts from the chimney from affecting the burner.

The draft hood can be built into the furnace cabinet (an internal draft diverter), or it could be installed separately above the top of the heating unit. If it is installed within the furnace cabinet, it becomes part of the manifold that collects all of the exhaust gases that come out of each cell of the exchanger.

Size of the Pool Heater

Determining whether the size of the heater is appropriate for the pool or spa that you're inspecting may or may not be within your inspection service. If it is, you should consider how a contractor sizes pool heaters for particular installations. There are a couple of different ways for a pool contractor to size a heater.

You should be aware of things other than BTU ratings. There are factors that influence the performance of a pool heater no matter what its size. A pool located in an extremely windy area can affect the performance of the heater because the wind may cause rapid cooling of the water. If the surface area of the pool is very large, that will increase evaporation and heat-loss rates. The volume of water is a main factor in determining the heater size, and irregularly-shaped containers are difficult to measure and attain an accurate calculation for, which is necessary in determining the heater size. The average temperature of the pool water that the heater starts at is a factor. The amount of shade over the pool could be a factor in the heater's performance. The average number of hours the pool heater is in use is a factor. The desired temperature in relation to the starting temperature (referred to as temperature rise) is another factor.

Most manufacturers of pool heaters provide information about calculating the size of the pool heater in relation to the surface area of the water being heated. About 100 BTUs every hour are needed for every 10 square feet of pool surface for every 1° of temperature rise desired.

A pool that is 15 feet wide by 20 feet long has a surface area of 300 square feet; 300 square feet divided by 10 square feet are 30 square feet; 30 square feet x 100 BTUs/1° = 3,000 BTUs for each degree of temperature rise desired. If you desire a 15° temperature rise, then 3,000 BTUs x 15° (rise) = 45,000 BTUs are needed every hour to maintain that desired water temperature. If you need that pool water maintained at the desired temperature all day, then 45,000 BTUs x 24 hours = 1,080,000 BTUs is the total for the day. But if you need the heater to maintain that water temperature only for about one-third of the day, then you can divide 45,000 BTUs by 3, so 45,000 BTUs ÷ 3 = 135,000 BTUs. For this example, a heater rated at least 135,000 BTUs would work. If a heat pump is installed, then at least a 9-ton heat pump would work, because 15,000 BTUs = about 1 ton-rating heat pump, and 135,000 ÷ 15,000 = 9.

This calculation works if you do not consider any other factors previously mentioned.

BTU stands for British thermal unit. The BTU is a unit of energy. It is approximately the amount of energy needed to heat 1 pound of water 1°. And there are 8.33 pounds of water in a gallon, and 7.5 gallons in each cubic foot of water.

Assume that you have a pool that is 15 feet wide by 20 feet long, and 4 feet deep (on average). Let's say that you need a temperature rise of 15° because the average temperature is 65° F and you want the pool water to be 80° F. You have 15 x 20 x 4 = 1,200 cubic feet (volume). Now, how many gallons are there in the pool? The answer is 1,200 x 7.5 gal./cu. ft. = 9,000 gallons. Now, how many pounds of water are in the pool (assuming there are about 8 pounds of water in a gallon)?

The answer is 9,000 gallons x 8 pounds = 72,000 pounds of water are in the pool. Now, how many BTUs will it take to raise the temperature of 72,000 pounds of water 15°? The answer is 72,000 x 15 = 1,080,000 BTUs, which is the same answer as the previous example-calculation.

Let's say that you wanted to know how long it would take for an existing pool heater to raise the temperature 15°. Take the heater's output-BTU rating and divide it by the number of pounds of water in the pool. Assume that the heater has a 180,000-BTU input rating, and a 135,000-BTU output rating (75% efficiency). We can calculate that 135,000 BTUs ÷ 72,000 pounds of water (9,000 gallons x 8 pounds) = 1.8° per hour. To raise the temperature 15°, it might take over eight hours (15° ÷ 1.8° per hour). Remember that to make the calculations easier, we're rounding the number of pounds of water in a gallon to 8, whereas the actual number is 8.33.

Let's say that you have a spa that is 5 feet round by 3 feet deep, and you want to raise the temperature 40°, from 60° F to 100° F. You don't have eight hours to wait for your hot tub to get hot! First, calculate the surface area. That's 3.14 x 2.5 x 2.5 = 19.6 square feet. Find the volume: 19.6 square feet x 3 feet deep = 59 cubic feet of water in your spa. Now, find out how many pounds of water there are in your tub: 59 cu. ft. x 7.5 gallons/cu. ft. x 8 lbs./gallon = 3,540 pounds of water in your hot tub. So, 3,540 pounds x 40° (rise) = 141,600 BTUs total. Your hot tub needs to have at least a 141,600-BTU heater. Remember that spa heaters are rated at BTUs per hour. That's a big heater for a small container of water. But you probably don't want to wait long for the tub to heat up. Spa heaters are typically doubled in size just to accommodate the expected needs of users.

It is recommended that the water temperature for a pool be set between 78° F and 82° F, and spas should be no hotter than 104° F. These temperatures may be recommended by your local plumbing code official.

Sizing spa heaters is generally based on how fast the spa needs to be heated to the desired temperature during a normal cycle. The tables below were adapted from information in *The Ultimate Guide to Pool Maintenance, 3rd Edition* by Terry Tamminen.

Pool Heater Size			
	10°	20°	30°
200 sq. ft.	21,000 BTUs	42,000 BTUs	63,000 BTUs
400 sq. ft.	42,000 BTUs	84,000 BTUs	126,000 BTUs
600 sq. ft.	63,000 BTUs	126,000 BTUs	189,000 BTUs
800 sq. ft.	84,000 BTUs	168,000 BTUs	252,000 BTUs
1,000 sq. ft.	105,000 BTUs	210,00 BTUs	315,000 BTUs

Spa Heater Size (per mins. needed for every 30° temperature rise desired)			
Spa Size	125,00 BTUs	250,000 BTUs	400,000 BTUs
200 gallons	30 minutes	15 minutes	less than 10 minutes
400 gallons	60 minutes	30 minutes	20 minutes
600 gallons	90 minutes	45 minutes	30 minutes
800 gallons	120 minutes	60 minutes	40 minutes
1,000 gallons	150 minutes	75 minutes	47 minutes

Section 12: Other Components and Devices

Timers

There are many different types and styles of timers. Hopefully, the instructions will be attached to the timer unit that you are inspecting. If you are not familiar with the timer device, it may be best to leave it alone. You may get complaints of malfunction that are often related to the timer if it is not properly returned to its original settings. You may inadvertently over-ride some functions if you are not familiar with it.

Time Clocks

A time clock is an important part of a pool system. A time clock controls when things turn on and operate during the day, including circulating the water through the filter, heating the water, and turning on lights at night. Many time clocks have 24-hour timers with on/off trippers. The trippers (also called dogs) are set to the time you want the unit to go on and off. Waterproof boxes of metal or plastic are available.

Twist Timers

Twist timers are used primarily for spas. The timer can usually go up to 60 minutes. There's a knob attached to a shaft that is twisted to the desired amount of time. By twisting the knob, a spring is wound. When it unwinds all the way, the electrical circuit is opened and the component is turned off.

Electronic Timers

Electronic timers are used for many spa and some pool equipment, including electronic thermostats and high-end controls. Electronic timers have backup batteries so that they don't lose their settings, including the time of day. Often, a problem with the pool can be caused by a bad battery. If you see unusual or no digital displays at a control unit, it may be that the battery needs to be replaced.

Remote Controls

Remote controls provide the means to operate devices of the pool or spa from a distance. With a remote control, you can turn on the pump, heater lights, or other things without having to go to the pool or spa. Some controls can be operated while you're in the pool. There are many different types of remote-control devices, but they all share some things in common. They all typically control the filter pump, jet pump, air blower, lights, heater, and other equipment. Typically, 110-volt electrical lines actually activate the equipment, whereas the low-voltage controls use wireless or sophisticated controls to activate certain devices.

There are two types of remote controls. One type uses air; the other uses electronics.

Air switches (or pneumatic switches) are generally found at the water's edge. There's no danger of electrocution because there are no conductive materials in the switch device. It's simply made of a push button on a long hose filled with air that, when compressed, activates a switch located near the equipment.

Electronic remote controls send signals wirelessly to a receiver that could be more than 1,000 feet away. The receiver is usually located near the pool equipment. It receives a radio signal from the remote and operates a certain device of the equipment.

A hard-wired remote control could be as simple as a toggle switch located inside the house that controls the spa pump and heater on/off switches.

Automatic controls are often complex because they do many things and offer many features to the user. The power center can consist of a control panel (or printed circuit board), relays, and circuit breakers. The outer box is typically waterproof, with a wiring diagram attached to the inside panel of the access door. The control panel of the power center is the heart of the automated pool system. Programming is done at the remote control in the house.

Air Blowers

An air blower, also called a bubbler or an air pump, introduces air into the spa water through a series of inlets. Many spas use the blower to provide massages. Spas can use it to mix air with water going through the jets. The air blower makes the bubbles. Air blowers for spas and hot tubs are essential to the experience. If there isn't an air blower installed for the spa jets, then you might find a PVC pipe sticking up out of the ground with an open slit cut into the top of it, providing a way for air to enter into the jet system.

Diving Boards

Diving boards at residential pools are not as popular today as they once were. As boards age, they need maintenance, repair and replacement. Most diving boards, unless they are new, will need repair or replacement. Most diving boards are made of wood covered with fiberglass, with a non-skid surface on the top. Some use a fulcrum or a spring. Some have cantilevered stands, fiberglass stands, or jump or spring boards.

Check for cracks in the fiberglass and wood rot underneath the fiberglass material. Diving boards should not appear to have been repaired. One of the only cosmetic repairs that should be noticeable is a new non-skid top. They tend to deteriorate with heavy use and UV exposure. Diving boards should look to be in great condition, without any flaws or concerns. If a diving board isn't in perfect condition, it may kill someone.

Check your local building codes to determine the requirements of the pool depth when a diving board is in place. The pool depth needs to be deep and large enough to ensure adequate room for safe diving. For small boards, the general rule of thumb is for the pool to be at least 10 feet deep, 15 feet wide, and 30 feet long, but those are very general numbers. Check your local codes because a client may look to you for some advice about safety.

Slides

Slides are typically made of fiberglass, with metal frames and steps. Similar to the general conditions for diving boards, the bigger (and higher) the slide, the bigger and deeper the pool needs to be.

Ladders

There are many different types of ladders and rails. Some are attached to only the deck, whereas some are secured to the pool-side or bottom. Look for loose connections where the ladder or rail connects to the masonry deck and pool floor. The cups or wedges sometimes come loose. The ladder needs to be sound, safe, and able to hold a person's weight.

Automatic Pool Cleaners

There are many different types and styles of automatic pool-cleaning devices. One common automatic pool cleaner is a robot-type, powered either by battery or by a long electrical line. It's like a vacuum sweeper that moves around automatically, sucking debris from the pool's bottom and sides. A small, computerized control board guides the robot around the pool.

A booster-pump cleaning system takes filtered pool water and pressurizes it in a separate pump, then sends the pressurized water through a hose to the vacuum cleaner that runs along the pool's bottom.

Another type is a vacuum cleaner that uses pressurized water and a long tail that agitates the bottom surface of the pool. The pressurized water also controls the unit and spins some wheels that aid in vacuuming.

Lighting

There are numerous types of high- and low-voltage lighting systems used to light pools, spas and surrounding areas. A typical pool or spa light is made up of a stainless-steel fixture. The fixture is installed in the wall of the pool or spa in a container called a light niche.

A light niche is a metal can that's big enough to hold a light fixture. It is cemented into the side of the pool and is intended to be watertight.

The electrical line enters the niche and goes into the fixture through waterproof seals. The lamp can be a standard 100-watt lamp (or bulb). In a spa, quartz or halogen bulbs may be used to provide the most light from a low-wattage lamp.

Don't turn on lights if they are not in direct contact with water. The lights are sealed tight and can easily overheat if not in contact with water.

Low-voltage lights use a transformer to drop the voltage from high 110-volt to low 24-volt. Low-voltage lights are commonly used in spas and fountains where you do not need very powerful lights.

You may find fiber optics being used for water lighting, but these are not very common.

Pool Covers

Pool covers help in retaining heat, reducing evaporation, and keeping debris out of the water. A pool requires less vacuuming if a cover is used to keep out the leaves and debris. Less energy is used to heat the pool if a cover is used to retain the heat. Heavy-duty covers with straps and/or locks can provide a layer of protection by preventing children from falling into spas and pools.

There are bubble covers, covers that roll out and back in, foam covers that are similar to bubble covers but are made of foam, and vinyl covers that are similar to bubble covers, but without the bubbles.

Bubble covers are commonly used. They are also called solar covers, sealed-air covers, and solar blankets. Bubble covers are made of two sheets of plastic. One side of the cover is smooth; the other is bumpy with bubbles. The sun warms the air bubbles, and the heat energy is transferred to the water in contact with the cover. Bubble covers should be laid on the water with the bubble-side down.

Pool-cover motors and controllers are usually located at the side of the pool in a box, or some type of recessed box with a flush cover. The storage box for the pool cover must have drainage provisions, and the motor should be totally enclosed and protected, and served by a GFCI circuit.

Quiz 10

1. T/F: Heat pumps cannot be used for pool heaters.

    ☐ True

    ☐ False

2. T/F: The heater shouldn't turn on unless the pump and motor are also going to be circulating water.

    ☐ True

    ☐ False

3. About _____ BTUs every hour are needed for every 10 square feet of pool surface for every 1° of temperature rise desired.

    ☐ 10

    ☐ 100

    ☐ 300

    ☐ 1,000

4. It is recommended that the water temperature for a pool be set between 78° F and ____° F, and spas should be no hotter than _____° F.

    ☐ 65..... 82

    ☐ 82..... 104

    ☐ 82..... 120

    ☐ 95..... 104

5. A(n) _____ is approximately the amount of energy needed to heat 1 pound of water 1°.

    ☐ Faraday unit

    ☐ potential

    ☐ BTU

    ☐ RTU

6. T/F: The storage box for the pool cover must have drainage provisions, and the motor should be totally enclosed and protected, and served by a GFCI circuit.

    ☐ True

    ☐ False

Answer Key is on page 86.

Section 13: Safety Barriers

Each year in the United States, about 300 children under the age of 5 drown in swimming pools, usually a pool owned by their family. In addition, more than 2,000 children in that age group are treated in hospital emergency rooms for submersion injuries. The following information can help families protect their young children around pools.

Most jurisdictions require some type of barrier at a pool and spa to prevent drowning. Sometimes, the barrier surrounds the pool but not the spa. Be sure not to overlook the issue of barriers when inspecting the spa.

An outdoor swimming pool, including an in-ground, above-ground, or on-ground pool, hot tub or spa, should be provided with a barrier that complies with the following standards:

1. The top of the barrier should be at least 48 inches above grade, measured on the side of the barrier that faces away from the swimming pool. The maximum vertical clearance between grade and the bottom of the barrier should be 4 inches, measured on the side of the barrier that faces away from the swimming pool. Where the top of the pool structure is above grade, such as an above-ground pool, the barrier may be at ground level, such as the pool structure, or mounted on top of the pool structure. Where the barrier is mounted on top of the pool structure, the maximum vertical clearance between the top of the pool structure and the bottom of the barrier should be 4 inches.

2. Openings in the barrier should not allow the passage of a 4-inch-diameter sphere.

3. Solid barriers that do not have openings, such as a masonry or stone wall, should not contain indentations or protrusions, except for normal construction tolerances and tooled masonry joints.

4. Where the barrier is composed of horizontal and vertical members, and the distance between the tops of the horizontal members is less than 45 inches, the horizontal members should be located on the swimming pool-side of the fence. Spacing between vertical members should not exceed 1¾ inches in width. Where there are decorative cutouts, spacing within the cutouts should not exceed 1¾ inches in width.

5. Where the barrier is composed of horizontal and vertical members, and the distance between the tops of the horizontal members is 45 inches or more, spacing between vertical members should not exceed 4 inches. Where there are decorative cutouts, spacing within the cutouts should not exceed 1¾ inches in width.

6. The maximum mesh size for chain-link fences should not exceed 1¾ inches square, unless the fence is provided with slats fastened at the top or the bottom, which reduce the openings to no more than 1¾ inches.

7. Where the barrier is composed of diagonal members, such as a lattice fence, the maximum opening formed by the diagonal members should be no more than 1¾ inches.

8. Access gates to the pool should comply with Section I, Paragraphs 1 through 7, and should be equipped to accommodate a locking device. Pedestrian access gates should open outward, away from the pool, and should be self-closing and have a self-latching device. Gates other than pedestrian access gates should have a self-latching device. Where the release mechanism of the self-latching device is located less than 54 inches from the bottom of the gate, (a) the release mechanism should be located on the pool-side of the gate at least 3 inches below the top of the gate, and (b) the gate and barrier should have no opening greater than ½-inch within 18 inches of the release mechanism.

9. Where a wall of a dwelling serves as part of the barrier, one of the following should apply:

   (a) All doors with direct access to the pool through that wall should be equipped with an alarm that produces an audible warning when the door and its screen, if present, are opened. The alarm should sound continuously for a minimum of 30 seconds within seven seconds after the door is opened. Alarms should meet the requirements of UL 2017 General-Purpose Signaling Devices and Systems, Section 77. The alarm should have a minimum sound-pressure rating of 85 dBA at 10 feet, and the sound of the alarm should be distinctive from other household sounds, such as smoke alarms, telephones and doorbells. The alarm should automatically reset under all conditions. The alarm should be equipped with manual means, such as touchpads or switches, to temporarily de-activate the alarm for a single opening of the door from either direction. Such de-activation should last for no more than 15 seconds. The de-activation touchpads or switches should be located at least 54 inches above the threshold of the door.

   (b) The pool should be equipped with a power safety cover that complies with ASTM F1346-91 listed below.

   (c) Other means of protection, such as self-closing doors with self-latching devices, are acceptable so long as the degree of protection afforded is not less than the protection afforded by (a) or (b) described above.

10. Where an above-ground pool structure is used as a barrier, or where the barrier is mounted on top of the pool structure, and the means of access is a ladder or steps, then:

   (a) the ladder to the pool or steps should be capable of being secured, locked or removed to prevent access; or

   (b) the ladder or steps should be surrounded by a barrier which meets Section I, Paragraphs 1 through 9. When the ladder or steps are secured, locked or removed, any opening created should not allow the passage of a 4-inch-diameter sphere.

Indoor Swimming Pool

All walls surrounding an indoor swimming pool should comply with Paragraph 9.

Barrier Locations

Barriers should be located so as to prohibit permanent structures, equipment and similar objects from being used to climb the barriers.

Exemptions

A portable spa with a safety cover that complies with ASTM F1346-91 is exempt from the guidelines presented here. But swimming pools, hot tubs, and non-portable spas with safety covers are not exempt from these provisions.

These guidelines on barriers have been adapted from information by the U.S. Consumer Product Safety Commission at **www.cpsc.gov**.

Quiz 11

1. The top of the barrier should be at least _____ inches above grade, measured on the side of the barrier that faces away from the swimming pool.

    ☐ 48

    ☐ 52

    ☐ 68

    ☐ 72

2. Openings in the barrier should not allow the passage of a _____-inch-diameter sphere.

    ☐ 1

    ☐ 2

    ☐ 3

    ☐ 4

3. Pedestrian access gates should open outward, away from the pool, and should have a(n) _____ device.

    ☐ auto-locking

    ☐ fire-resistant

    ☐ self-latching

    ☐ steel

Answer Key is on page 86.

Section 14: Water Chemistry

Water has a natural tendency to balance itself. If pool or spa water has little dissolved solids, then the water will aggressively try to balance itself by causing things that come in contact with it to dissolve into solution. Water is a universal solvent. Over time, it will dissolve anything. The water will attack tile, grout, concrete, iron, copper, etc. When the water is balanced, it no longer attacks. If the water has too much dissolved solids, then the water will aggressively try to balance itself by dropping calcium carbonate out of the solution, resulting in deposits of hard precipitate called calcium carbonate or scale. Water chemistry is all about achieving balance.

There are several factors involved in achieving balance. They are:

- pH;
- total alkalinity;
- calcium hardness;
- temperature; and
- TDS, or total dissolved solids.

The pH should be between 7.4 and 7.6. Total alkalinity should be maintained in the range of 80 to 150 ppm. An acceptable level of calcium hardness for a plaster pool is generally considered to be about 250 ppm. The total dissolved solids should be no more than 1,500 ppm for pools and spas.

pH

pH is the single most important element in a swimming pool's water chemistry. It affects every other chemical balance in pool water. pH stands for *potens hydrogen*, which, translated from Latin, means the "power of hydrogen."

pH is a measure of the hydrogen ion (H+) concentration in water. It indicates the relative acidity or basicity of pool water. pH is measured on a scale of 0 (strong acid) to 14 (strong base), with 7 being the neutral pH. The lower the pH, the more acidic the solution. The pH scale is logarithmic, which means that a small change in pH actually represents a big change in acidity. Water that is 6 pH is ten times more acidic than water that is 7 pH.

The acceptable range for pools is 7.2 to 7.8. In pools and spas, a slightly alkaline pH of 7.4 to 7.6 is most desirable because this range is most comfortable to human eyes, and provides for optimum use of free chlorine while maintaining water that is not corrosive or scale-forming. The pH of a human tear is about 7.5.

What if pH is too low (below 7)?

- Water becomes acidic.
- Chlorine residuals dissipate rapidly.
- Eye irritation occurs.
- Plaster walls become etched.
- Metal fittings, the pump impeller, and the heater core may corrode.
- Dissolved metals may leave stains on walls.
- There will be a rapid loss of alkalinity.

What if pH is too high (above 8)?

- Chlorine activity is slowed and inefficient.
- Scales will form and discolor pool walls.
- Water becomes cloudy.
- The filter is overworked.
- Eye irritation may occur.

pH Adjustment

To avoid these problems, the pH must be maintained between 7.2 and 7.8. The most desirable level for pH is between 7.4 and 7.6.

There are many factors that affect the pH of pool and spa water, including:

- human waste;
- disinfectants;
- fresh water;
- airborne debris;
- water-balance chemicals;
- aeration; and
- evaporation.

Controlling pH

Controlling pH is essential for making the pool comfortable and clean, and for protecting the pool equipment. To control pH, the proper level of alkalinity must be maintained. Testing the total alkalinity should be done prior to changing (raising or lowering) the pH.

Increasing the pH

The pH can be raised by adding soda ash or sodium carbonate (Na_2CO_3). Never add more than 2 pounds per 10,000 gallons in a single treatment. Be sure the pump is running when chemicals are added. Allow the water to re-circulate, then re-test it to determine if further treatment is necessary. Caustic soda (sodium hydroxide) is sometimes used with chemical feed pumps to raise pH. If problems with low pH persist, it may be necessary to raise total alkalinity to stabilize the pH.

Lowering the pH

To lower the pH, you need to add acid or acid salts. A common liquid acid used is muriatic acid. Muriatic acid (HCI or hydrochloric acid) or sodium bisulfate ($NaHSO_4$) lowers the pH. Sulfuric acid (H_2SO_4) is available in some areas. Carefully add acid at the deep end of the pool. Try not to pour acid near pool walls or fittings. Remember: When using or diluting acids, add the acid to the water. Never add water to acid.

Factors That Affect pH	
Lowers pH	**Raises pH**
acid	soda ash
gas chlorine	sodium hypochlorite
trichlor chlorine	calcium hypochlorite
dichlor chlorine	caustic soda
rainwater	bicarbonate of soda
aluminum	swimmer waste
organic litter	algae growth
make-up water	make-up water

Effects of Low pH	**Effects of High pH**
corrosive water	scaley water
irritation of the eyes	cloudy water
metals corrode	filters get clogged
walls get stained	heater elements get clogged

Effects of Low pH	Effects of High pH
chlorine loss	circulation could be reduced
etching of pool surface	chlorine is not effective
vinyl liners get wrinkles	irritation of the eyes and skin

Total Alkalinity (TA)

Total alkalinity is closely associated with pH. It is the measure of the water's ability to resist changes in pH. It is like an anchor that wants to keep the water's pH where it should be. Expressed in parts per million (ppm), total alkalinity is the result of alkaline materials, including carbonates, bicarbonates and hydroxides, but mostly bicarbonates. This acid-neutralizing (buffering) capacity of water is desirable because it helps prevent large variations in pH whenever small amounts of acid or alkali are added to the pool. A pH bounce happens when the pH level rapidly moves up and down with the addition of chemicals.

Total alkalinity should be maintained in the range of 80 to 150 ppm.

If total alkalinity is too low:

 • pH changes rapidly when chemicals or impurities enter the water. The pH may drop rapidly, causing etching and corrosion.

If total alkalinity is too high:

 • pH becomes difficult to adjust. High pH often causes other problems, such as cloudy water, decreased disinfectant effectiveness, scale formation, and filter problems.

Total alkalinity can be raised by the addition of bicarbonate of soda (sodium bicarbonate or baking soda). The addition of 1.4 pounds bicarbonate of soda per 10,000 gallons will raise total alkalinity 10 ppm.

In some cases, soda ash can be used to raise total alkalinity. Pound for pound, soda ash raises alkalinity 60% more than sodium bicarbonate, and it is cheaper than sodium bicarbonate. The problem with using soda ash to increase alkalinity is that it drastically increases pH. This can cause cloudy water and scale formation. Soda ash should be used only to increase total alkalinity if you also need to increase the pH, or if only a small increase in alkalinity is needed.

Chemical manufacturers produce a total-alkalinity increaser, which combines the effects of sodium bicarbonate and soda ash. The product, called sodium sesquicarbonate or sodium hydrogen carbonate, affects total alkalinity more than sodium bicarbonate but does not cause quite the increase in pH that soda ash does.

Total alkalinity can be lowered by adding muriatic acid or sodium bisulfate. Acid may be added in doses of up to 1 quart per 10,000 gallons. Total-alkalinity tests can be made and acid can added every two hours.

Calcium Hardness

When water comes into contact with masonry and rock that contain calcium and magnesium, the water tends to dissolve these minerals into the water. When water has a low calcium content, it aggressively tries to dissolve calcium carbonate from anything in contact with it. Calcium carbonate is a main ingredient in pool tile, cement and plaster. Corrosive water will etch these finish surfaces in a pool.

Calcium hardness is a measure of the dissolved calcium salts in the water, or the amount of calcium carbonate ($CaCO_3$). Total hardness is the sum of calcium and magnesium.

"Soft" and "hard" water refer to the amount of calcium in the water. Low calcium-hardness levels in spas contribute to foaming. Low calcium hardness in pools causes etching of surfaces.

An ideal level for calcium hardness is 200 to 400 ppm.

Calcium carbonate is likely to occur where there is water evaporation or high temperatures. Scale is a crusty, white deposit that can cause a pool surface to feel very rough. Scale can reduce circulation flow, attach to a heater's exchanger, and clog the filter and pipes. Usually, high pH and alkalinity with high levels of calcium hardness will result in scale formation.

Under normal conditions, this should not be a problem in properly-operated swimming pools. Estimates of the proper range of calcium hardness vary widely, but the ideal level for a plaster pool is generally considered to be about 250 ppm. If calcium hardness is very low, then water may leach calcium from pool walls, causing pitting and etching of the plaster surface. Very high calcium hardness may contribute to scale formation and clouding of the water.

To raise calcium hardness, calcium chloride ($CaCl_2$) can be added.

To lower calcium hardness, anhydrous trisodium phosphate may be used. One pound of trisodium phosphate per 10,000 gallons of water will lower calcium hardness by 11 ppm. Use it in small increments, or clouding may occur. Another method of lowering calcium hardness is to simply drain off part of the pool water and dilute the remaining water with fresh make-up water.

Scum Line

The scum line refers to the deposits that form at and above the water line. A thin film of water on the wall's surface can evaporate, leaving deposits of chemicals above the water line. The deposits could come from calcium scale, skin, suntan oil, cosmetics, etc.

Temperature

Temperature becomes a significant factor in extreme conditions. In spas with water temperatures hotter than 104° F, there's an increased tendency for scaling to develop. At water temperatures lower than 32° F, scaling could also occur.

Total Dissolved Solids (TDS)

After a pool has been in use for some time, dissolved solids may begin to accumulate. These unfilterable solids include bodily waste, suntan lotion, stabilizers, chlorines, defoamers, algicide, dirt, metal, stain-control chemicals, pollen, etc. TDS is the total weight of all soluble matter in the water. Excessively high levels of TDS will cause the water to be "tired" or look dull.

Normally, this is less of a problem with outdoor pools because of rainwater and lack of use during winter months. Indoor pools sometimes have a buildup of dissolved solids, which requires draining the pool and refilling it with fresh water. Most pools should be drained after three to five years.

It is generally recommended that TDS should be under 1,500 ppm.

Testing

Determining whether the water of a pool or spa is in balance requires testing using a full water-chemistry analysis. If the water is not balanced, adjustments must be made.

Testing validates water quality and guides changes that must be made to the water to protect the bathers and the equipment.

There are four basic methods used to test pool and spa water:

- colorimetric, which relies on color matching;
- titrimetric, which determines the unknown concentration of a chemical by using a concentration of a known re-agent;
- turbidimetric, which is a measure of how many solids are suspended in the water; and
- electronic.

There are many types of tests that can be performed at a pool, but the most common factors to test for are:

- disinfectant and pH;
- total alkalinity;
- calcium hardness;
- TDS;
- and many other elements, including nitrates, phosphates and metals.

The pool technician might want to test the pool for residual disinfectant and disinfectant byproducts, such as chlorine and bromine. These are important tests.

The pool industry has developed an index to determine whether the water is balanced in relation to calcium carbonate. The Saturation Index (SI) is a method of finding out whether the water will deposit calcium or maintain it in solution. The SI can be used in testing the water and making adjustments to put the water into a balanced state.

Disinfection

Disinfection is used to destroy micro-organisms that might cause human disease. Many things can affect the disinfection process in pools and spas, including the pH, bodily waste, contamination, and temperature. As these factors increase, it becomes more difficult to keep disinfection of the water maintained.

Disinfectant is sometimes called sanitizer. Disinfectants kill or inactivate 99.9% or more of the micro-organisms that cause disease (pathogens). Some pathogens are not alive and cannot be killed; therefore, the term "inactivate" is used.

A proper balance of the previously described water-chemistry factors will provide water that will not damage pool components and is not irritating to swimmers. It is necessary to provide for disinfection of the water to prevent the spread of disease organisms from person to person, and to prevent unwanted growth of bacteria and algae in the pool.

Chlorine

The most commonly-used disinfectant for swimming pools is chlorine (hypochlorous acid). In its elemental form, chlorine is a heavy, greenish-yellow gas that is so toxic that it has been used as a weapon in chemical warfare. Because of the extremely high potential for injury or death from improper use of chlorine gas, many chlorine compounds have been formulated to provide chlorine in forms that can be handled and used safely by swimming pool operators.

Liquid chlorine and muriatic acids are generally sold in 1-gallon plastic bottles. When pouring chlorine into the pool, the bottle should be held very close to the water surface to prevent splashing. The chlorine should be added near a return line while the pump is circulating. Chlorine should never be poured into a skimmer.

Sanitizers, acids and alkaline products are available in granular form. Chlorine tablets, called floaters or ducks, are available, too.

The following forms of chlorine are commonly used in swimming pools:

Gas Chlorine: 100% Available Chlorine	
Advantages	**Disadvantages**
cheapest form of chlorine	extremely dangerous
no residue from carriers	special room needed for chlorine
xxx	feed equipment is expensive
xxx	special training and safety equipment are needed
xxx	lowers pH; must constantly add pH increaser

Because of the special hazards associated with the use of gaseous chlorine, its use has been prohibited at public swimming pools in many areas.

Calcium Hypochlorite: Granular or Pelletized, 65% Available Chlorine	
Advantages	**Disadvantages**
relatively cheap	not stabilized; loses strength if not covered
can be mixed into solution	does not dissolve completely; leaves residue
xxx	high pH (11.7); raises pH of pool
xxx	highly reactive; may cause fires

Sodium Hypochlorite: Liquid Bleach, 12.5% Available Chlorine	
Advantages	**Disadvantages**
cheap	bulky and heavy
no dissolving required; no residue	not stabilized; loses strength rapidly
xxx	high pH (10-13); raises pH of pool
xxx	highly reactive; may cause fires

Free chlorine residual is the amount of chlorine in the pool that has not reacted with substances other than water. It is the chlorine that is available to disinfect pool water and oxidize organic substances. Free chlorine residual should be maintained between 1 and 3 ppm.

Combined chlorine is chlorine in the pool that has reacted with substances other than water and is no longer available in its free state. Some combined chlorines are bactericides, but they contribute little to the disinfection process. Chlorine combined with ammonia produces chloramines that cause eye irritation and an objectionable chlorine odor. For this reason, combined chlorine residual should be kept to a minimum -- preferably, below 0.2 ppm.

Total chlorine residual is the concentration of free chlorine plus combined chlorine. To determine the combined chlorine residual, test for free chlorine and total chlorine:

total chlorine minus free chlorine = combined chlorine.

Breakpoint chlorination is the process by which combined chlorine and some organics are "burned out" of the pool by the addition of large amounts of chlorine. The reaction of chlorine with ammonia to form chloramines occurs in several stages, with free chlorine consumed at each stage. If enough chlorine is added to the water, the total chlorine residual will rise to a point that forces the reaction of chlorine with ammonia to go rapidly to completion. Compounds of nitrogen and chlorine are released from the water, and the apparent residual chlorine decreases. The point at which the chlorine residual suddenly drops is called the breakpoint. When enough chlorine is added to pass the breakpoint, combined chlorine compounds disappear, the potential for eye irritation and chlorine odors disappear, and the chlorine remaining in the water is all in its free state.

Super-chlorination: In order to prevent buildup of chloramines in the pool, it is necessary to periodically add large amounts of new chlorine in an effort to pass the breakpoint. Public swimming pools should be super-chlorinated about once a week. The amount of chlorine needed to reach the breakpoint will vary, depending on the amount of organic material introduced by bathers, and the level of free chlorine maintained in the pool. If the amount of combined chlorine is known, then the amount of new chlorine needed is 10 times the amount of combined chlorine. When the combined chlorine residual is not known, super-chlorination is accomplished by adding 10 ppm of new chlorine to the pool. Ordinarily, calcium hypochlorite at a dose of at least 1 pound per 10,000 gallons is used for super-chlorination.

Non-Chlorine Shock Treatments

Several products have been developed that oxidize organics without the use of chlorine. Pool operators who use such products can accomplish the reduction of organics without closing the pool for any longer than it takes to dissolve and distribute the chemicals. These products are more expensive than chlorine, but may be preferred where it is necessary to keep a pool open.

Bromine

Bromine is chemically very similar to chlorine. Bromine compounds tend to react more slowly than chlorine compounds, so bromine is generally more stable and less subject to dissipation in sunlight. The dissociation of hypobromous acid into the bromine ion is less affected by pH than the corresponding reaction of chlorine. This makes bromine active over a larger range of pH than chlorine. Bromine will combine with ammonia to form bromamines similar to chlorine but, unlike chloramines, bromamines are effective bactericides and do not produce the degree of odor and eye irritation associated with chloramines. Bromine is less affected by high temperature and nitrogen wastes than chlorine, so it is particularly attractive for use in hot-water spas. Bromine is more expensive than chlorine and has not yet received widespread acceptance by swimming pool operators.

The form of bromine most commonly used in pools and spas is the organic chemical bromo-chloro-dimethylhydantoin that contains both bromine and chlorine. It comes in tablet form for use in erosion feeders.

Algae

Algae are tiny plants that bloom and grow in swimming pools if nutrients are present and a sufficient level of free chlorine is not maintained. Algae propagate by airborne spores. They enter swimming pools and quickly turn the water green. When conditions favor their growth, they can cause black and/or green spots on pool walls. Heavy rain, intense sunlight, and the presence of nitrogenous material all contribute to "algae bloom," as the rapid growth of algae is called. Sometimes, algae bloom results in a sharp rise in pH, as the algae consume carbon dioxide in the pool water. If algae bloom is present, super-chlorination should be used. Then, using an algaecide will control it and prevent its reoccurrence. The best insurance against algae is to maintain a free-chlorine residual in the pool at all times. An effective way to do this is to sanitize with stabilized pool-chlorinating concentrates, and add algaecide according to the directions on the label.

Below are descriptions of the three most common algae problems in swimming pools.

Green algae are the most common algae in swimming pools. They float in water and coat pool surfaces. Left unchecked, green algae will very quickly turn the pool water pea-green.

Mustard algae settle on pool walls and cause a slimy, yellow film.

Black algae appear in "buds" or clumps attached to tile grout, corners, steps and pool surfaces.

Green algae are very susceptible to chemical treatment, so super-chlorinate with 10 to 20 ppm chlorine in the evening. Keep the filter running, and brush the pool's walls and bottom. Periodically check the chlorine level, and maintain it above 3 ppm until the water clears. Using an algaecide-containing quaternary ammonia the next morning will help prevent the return of green algae.

Mustard algae are much more resistant to chemical treatment and cling more stubbornly to pool walls than green algae. Adjust the pH and super-chlorinate as similarly done for green algae, then brush diligently. Later, vacuum the pool, check the chlorine level, and super-chlorinate again, if necessary. Mustard algae will generally return unless treated with a special mustard algaecide or a copper-based algaecide. Algaecide should be added in the morning to treat algae in daylight, which is its most active period.

Black algae are very difficult to get rid of. They can be controlled to some extent by frequent super-chlorination, and diligent brushing with a stiff brush. Spot-treatments can be made by turning off the recirculation pumps and pouring granular chlorine directly on recently brushed spots. Trichlor tablets can also be rubbed on recently brushed areas to spot-treat. Black algae can usually be controlled with the use of strong algaecides and maintenance with relatively high free-chlorine residual, but complete removal of black algae may require draining and cleaning the pool.

Section 15: Repairs Needed

Check the pool for plaster cracks, blisters, popped-off areas, and delamination. Some areas can be very small (about the size of a dime) to very big (about the size of a stop sign). These areas can be repaired. If there are damaged areas bigger than that, then re-plastering may be required. The causes of delamination may likely be from an imbalance in the water, making the water aggressive enough to take calcium out of the plaster. When calcium is taken from the plaster, the plaster becomes weak and starts to separate or delaminate.

Check for delaminated or blistered areas of plaster by tapping with the handle of a screwdriver. Listen for hollow sounds. Ideally, this type of inspection takes place when the water is drained from the pool. It is very challenging to identify defects in the plaster when the pool is filled with water.

Sometimes, the rebar inside the concrete will bleed through the concrete and plaster. It will appear as red spots or streaks in the plaster. These steel bleeds could occur in the pool floor or walls. It is often the rebar ties that actually cause the problem. The ties can be too close to the plaster surface, so the tie will actually wick water toward the rebar.

Tiles can crack and pop off. Coping tiles and stones can, too. A coping stone that is loose or has raised up might be an indication of a significant issue underneath the stone, such as settlement or heaving problems.

Section 16: Commercial Pools

There aren't many significant differences between commercial and residential pools and spas. Commercial pools and equipment are simply bigger.

Commercial pools are typically considered to be pools that are used by the public, or any pool other than a private one. They are dealt with in a serious manner in order to protect the public health. Health departments mandate rules and stringent regulations for commercial pools. Most jurisdictions and local authorities enforce rules about testing and maintaining healthy water, signage, pool covers, safety equipment, and turnover rates. Health inspectors commonly visit public pools and spas once or twice a year.

Some of the main differences between standard residential pools and large commercial pools are the safety signs that are required, the larger equipment, and the extra pressure gauges. The commercial pool could simply be 10 to 20 times the size of a residential one. Large public pools don't have one or two skimmers, but skimmers that run the entire perimeter of the pool. The commercial skimmer is not very different than a residential one, but it's a lot bigger.

An important factor in commercial pools is the bather-load calculations. Most jurisdictions limit the number of bathers per square foot of a commercial pool. It is important for the commercial pool technician to calculate and post the bather loads, considering how much water can be displaced by 100 bathers in a public pool.

The equipment that commercial pools use is simply bigger than that used in residential applications. The equipment and components are built with heavy-duty materials and increased capacities.

Commercial pools use surge tanks. A surge tank collects the water that is displaced from heavy bather loads. When bathers leave the pool, the water level drops, and the water inside the surge tank is pumped back into the pool, along with some new water.

A slurry feeder is commonly used at commercial pool filters. A slurry feeder is a big bucket in which a slurry of DE is mixed with water and is used in the commercial filter. The commercial filter is one of the same types used for a residential pool: DE, cartridge, or sand.

The most commonly-used form of sanitizer for a commercial pool is chlorine gas. It is efficient and the least expensive. However, chlorine gas is not used in residential pools. To reduce the risks of poisoning from chlorine's high acute toxicity, the U.S. Environmental Protection Agency (EPA) requires that its use in non-residential pools be restricted to certified pesticide applicators.

Commercial pools have equipment rooms. That room must be kept clean and dry. There must be no chemicals stored in the equipment room. A sump pump should be installed in the equipment room to handle any serious leakage problem. Chemicals for a commercial pool must be stored in a separate room that is located and well-ventilated, with signs posted outside on the door.

The local building codes dictate signage. Signs are required for commercial pools, including maximum bather loads, warning signs about diving, lifeguard signs, rules for the pool and spa, etc.

Quiz 12

1. _____ is the single most important element in a swimming pool's water chemistry.

☐ Hp

☐ pH

☐ TDS

☐ Temperature

2. If the pH is too _____, the water becomes cloudy.

☐ high

☐ low

☐ hot

☐ neutral

3. T/F: To avoid problems with water quality, pH must be maintained between 7.2 and 7.8.

☐ True

☐ False

4. There aren't many significant differences between commercial and residential pools and spas; commercial pools and equipment are simply _____.

☐ bigger

☐ smaller

5. T/F: Commercial pools use surge tanks.

☐ True

☐ False

6. T/F: Signs are not required for commercial pools.

☐ True

☐ False

Answer Key is on page 86.

Section 17: InterNACHI® Pool & Spa Inspection Checklist

This basic inspection checklist is part of InterNACHI's free, online "How to Inspect Pools and Spas" Course at **www.nachi.org/pool-spa-course**.

To have adequate and functional water flow through the pool system, there are several things that need to be in good shape:

- There has to be enough water in the pool or spa. Check the level of the water.
- There shouldn't be any water leaks at the plumbing connections or equipment.
- All of the valves should be fully open.
- There shouldn't be any trapped air in the system. Air at the filter tank should be purged routinely.
- The skimmer and main drain should be clear of blockages and debris. Skimmers require cleaning.
- The strainer pot at the pump should be cleaned routinely.
- There might be an imbalance of the water chemistry, causing scaling. Check for scale-causing clogging or restriction of water flow.
- The heater should be on and activated. The gas shut-off valve should be open. The switch should be on. Check for a pilot light, ignition, or flame at the fuel-fired heater. Check the level in the propane storage tank.
- The thermostat should be connected, active, and set properly.

NSPF Pool & Spa Inspection Checklist

The following inspection checklist was adapted from the guidelines recommended by the National Swimming Pool Foundation (NSPF). Use the checklist as a starting point in developing your own checklist that fits your inspection procedure and needs.

The inspector should check for the following:

- Adequate fencing, gates, barriers, alarms, and/or other protective devices are installed.
- Adequate storage space is provided for equipment.
- Decks around pool are not cluttered.
- The pool is covered when not in use.
- Surfaces leading to the pool, including the deck and steps, are slip-resistant.
- Decks on all sides of the pool meet minimum safety standards.
- The deck is separated from the pool wall perimeter.
- There are no standing puddles on the deck.
- All ladders, stanchions, chairs, and rails have treads with a contrasting color coating or tile on both the top and vertical rise.
- No unpleasant odors or irritating fumes are apparent.
- No physical damage is apparent at the pool equipment.
- Main drain grates are bolted securely to the pool's bottom.
- Grates are visible from the deck, with no apparent damage.

- Drain covers are installed.
- Water return inlets are installed.
- The pool is vacuumed daily.
- No debris is visible. The water is clean.
- There's no discoloration of the water.
- There is no visible algae growth.
- The pool water is tested at the frequency required or desired.
- All water quality and chemical levels were within acceptable ranges as of the most current test.
- Bacteriological water analysis is performed on a regular basis.
- The water temperature is maintained within acceptable levels and is appropriate for the primary activities being conducted in the pool.
- The water temperature has been measured and recorded.
- The type of heater is identified.
- The efficiency and BTU ratings of the heater are identified.
- The heater is installed on a level, non-combustible base.
- Safety devices are installed on the heater.
- The thermostat is located and identified.
- Check valves between the heater and filter are installed.
- Bonding and grounding are visible.
- The heater is installed downstream of the pump and filter.
- A solar-heating system is installed.
- The solar-heating system type is identified.
- The solar-heating system is active.
- Pool chemicals are stored a safe distance away from the heater.
- Adequate clearances around the heater are maintained.
- Coping stones and tiles are not chipped, cracked or loose.
- The pool shell appears smooth, without readily visible defects.
- There is no visible surface staining.
- The water level appears to be maintained to allow for the removal of floating debris.
- The water level appears at the proper height to allow continuous overflow of water into the gutters or skimmers.
- Skimmer weirs, skimmer baskets, deck covers, and flow-adjustment devices are installed.
- Lights are installed and are operational.
- The type, number and wattage of deck lighting are identified.
- The number of underwater lights is noted.
- GFCIs are installed.
- Electrical wiring is not passing directly over the pool or spa.
- Hose bibs are installed near the pool.

- No apparent defects or signs of repair are observed at the diving board.
- The manufacturer of the diving board is visible on the board itself.
- The centrifugal pump is secured to its base and is operating quietly.
- The hair and lint strainer basket is clean of debris.
- The type of pipe has been identified.
- Pipes and fittings are not leaking.
- Pipes are supported adequately.
- Pipes are not showing signs of calcification, corrosion or deterioration.
- Air pressure-relief valves are installed on all pressure filter tanks.
- Filter tanks are accessible.
- The filter's brand is identified.
- A clean sight glass or visual outfall of at least 3 feet has been provided.
- The pressurized filter tanks and hair and lint traps are not leaking and are properly sealed.
- All piping, filters and components that are part of the system are labeled, tagged, color-coded, or otherwise identified.
- A spa is installed.
- The spa is operational.
- A spa cover is installed.
- No physical damage is apparent at the spa.
- A spa timer is installed and not reachable by a spa user.
- The emergency shut-off switch for the spa is installed and clearly labeled.
- The spa appears clean and adequately maintained.

California: Seven Safety Features

In some areas, such as California, there are certain pool features that home inspectors are required to inspect. Those features are listed below. In California, the swimming pool or spa must be equipped with at least two of the following seven drowning-prevention safety features:

1. an enclosure that isolates the swimming pool or spa from the private single-family home;

2. removable mesh fencing that meets American Society for Testing and Materials (ASTM) Specification F2286 standards in conjunction with a gate that is self-closing and self-latching and can accommodate a key-lockable device;

3. an approved safety pool cover;

4. exit alarms on the private single-family home's doors that provide direct access to the swimming pool or spa. The exit alarm may cause either an alarm noise or a verbal warning, such as a repeating notification that "the door to the pool is open";

5. a self-closing, self-latching device with a release mechanism placed no lower than 54 inches above the floor on the private single-family home's doors, providing direct access to the swimming pool or spa;

6. an alarm that, when placed in a swimming pool or spa, will sound upon detection of accidental or unauthorized entrance into the water. The alarm shall meet and be independently certified to the ASTM Standard F2208 "Standard Safety Specification for Residential Pool Alarms," which includes surface motion, pressure, sonar, laser, and infrared type alarms. A swimming protection alarm feature designed for individual use, including an alarm feature designed for individual use, including an alarm attached to a child that sounds when the child exceeds a certain distance or becomes submerged in water, is not a qualifying drowning prevention safety feature; and

7. other means of protection, if the degree of protection afforded is equal to or greater than that afforded by any of the features set forth above and has been independently verified by an approved testing laboratory as meeting standards for those features established by the ASTM or the American Society of Mechanical Engineers (ASME).

Section 18: Maintenance Schedule

- Check the water level once a day.
- Check the pH twice a week.
- Check hardness, TDS, and total alkalinity once a month.
- Test for metals once every six months.
- Check the skimmer basket twice a week.
- Check the pump strainer pot once a week.
- Look for leaks every day.
- Vacuum the pool once or twice a week.
- Brush the pool walls and bottom once a week.
- Clean the water line once a week.
- Clean the solar panels once a month.
- Empty and clean the filter every three months.
- Winterize once a year.

Appendix I: Answer Keys

Answer Key for Quiz 1

1. A swimming pool is a permanent structure in the ground, or partially in the ground, that is capable of holding water with a depth greater than **42** inches outside a building.

2. T/F: A hot tub or spa moves and changes water in way similar to that of a pool.
   Answer: **True**

3. There are **7.5** gallons of water in 1 cubic foot of water.

4. T/F: "1 ppm" means one part mixed with a million parts.
   Answer: **True**

5. One gallon of water weighs **8.3** pounds.

Answer Key for Quiz 2

1. The most common in-ground pool shell is made of **concrete**.

2. Most **spas** are made of fiberglass or acrylic, unless they are designed and built on-site.

3. An above-ground pool should be level within **1 inch**.

4. The top part of a pool wall is called the **bond beam**, which supports the coping and edge around the pool.

5. T/F: The pool's surface plaster cannot be of any color other than white.
   Answer: **False**

Answer Key for Quiz 3

1. To understand how a pool or spa works, you can follow the path that the **water** takes in a pool or spa system.

2. T/F: Main drains are usually located at the shallowest part of a pool.
   Answer: **False**

3. T/F: The main drain should be visually inspected regularly (ideally, daily), particularly when the pool is being serviced or when the pool floor is being swept.
   Answer: **True**

4. The highest concentration of contamination is located at the **surface** of the pool.

5. Most skimmers have **weirs**, which are the small floating, hinged devices that allow water to enter the skimmer.

6. T/F: The Virginia Graeme Baker Pool and Spa Safety Act was designed to prevent the tragic and hidden hazard of drain entrapments and eviscerations in pools and spas.
   Answer: **True**

Answer Key for Quiz 4

1. The **pump** is the heart of the circulation system, and the pipes are the veins and arteries.

2. **PVC** piping and fittings are commonly used for residential swimming pools.

3. Schedule **40** PVC pipe is commonly used for pool plumbing.

4. Once the water is filtered and heated, it must be returned to the pool or spa through the **return inlets**.

Answer Key for Quiz 5

1. Manual 3-port valves function following the shape of the letter **Y**, where the flow of water can come up from the stem and be controlled and diverted to either or both branches.

2. T/F: Three-port valves are typically found if the pool and spa are connected to the same single pump, filter and heating system.
Answer: **True**

3. A **ball** valve can be totally open, totally closed, or any position in between.

4. A **gate** valve permits you to completely stop, but not modulate, the flow within a pipe, and should not be used in a partially open or partially closed position.

5. **Unions** allow a contractor to remove and replace equipment without installing new plumbing.

Answer Key for Quiz 6

1. T/F: The best idea is to have the water heated by the pool heater before going to the solar panels
Answer: **False**

2. The most common type of solar heating system is a(n) **open**-loop system.

3. T/F: A common maintenance issue is debris and dirt collecting on the panels.
Answer: **True**

4. A(n) **closed**-loop solar heating system is one that is separate from the pool water.

Answer Key for Quiz 7

1. The **pump** is what moves the water, and the **motor** is what turns electricity into mechanical energy.

2. The **impeller** moves the water by spinning.

3. Attached to the pump is the **strainer pot**, which filters out and traps small debris, such as hair.

4. **Cavitation** is a symptom of a problem which can occur when the impeller doesn't have enough water.

5. The **turnover** rate of a pool refers to how long it takes for all of the water inside the pool to circulate once through the entire system, including the filter.

6. T/F: A bad pool motor will tell you that it's bad by the way it sounds.
Answer: **True**

Answer Key for Quiz 8

1. T/F: A swimmer floating in the pool, not touching anything but the surrounding water, could become part of a fault-current path.
   Answer: **True**

2. A **dry**-niche luminaire is installed behind a window below the water level and does not allow any water penetration.

3. The **wet**-niche luminaire fixture is designed to have water completely surrounding it.

4. All 15- and 20-ampere, single-phase, 125-volt receptacles located within 20 feet of the inside walls of the pool and spa shall be protected by a(n) **GFCI**.

5. T/F: There should be no switches (including timers or panelboards) within 5 feet horizontally from the inside walls of pools, spas or hot tubs, except where separated by a barrier.
   Answer: **True**

6. **Equipotential** bonding is joining metallic parts to form an electrically conductive path that will result in electrical continuity between components to ensure that the electrical potential will be the same throughout.

7. The bonding conductor should be at least **8** AWG or larger solid copper.

Answer Key for Quiz 9

1. T/F: There are three general types of filters you might find at a pool or spa: sand and gravel; DE; and cartridge.
   Answer: **True**

2. T/F: Of all the filter types, sand filters are the most efficient.
   Answer: **False**

3. **Cartridge** filters are ones in which pool water passes through cartridges of fine-mesh, pleated fabric.

4. **Backwashing** is a way to clean a sand pool filter.

Answer Key for Quiz 10

1. T/F: Heat pumps cannot be used for pool heaters.
   Answer: **False**

2. T/F: The heater shouldn't turn on unless the pump and motor are also going to be circulating water.
   Answer: **True**

3. About **100** BTUs every hour are needed for every 10 square feet of pool surface for every 1° of temperature rise desired.

4. It is recommended that the water temperature for a pool be set between 78° F and **82°** F, and spas should be no hotter than **104°** F.

5. A(n) **BTU** is approximately the amount of energy needed to heat 1 pound of water 1°.

6. T/F: The storage box for the pool cover must have drainage provisions, and the motor should be totally enclosed and protected, and served by a GFCI circuit.
   Answer: **True**

Answer Key for Quiz 11

1. The top of the barrier should be at least **48** inches above grade, measured on the side of the barrier that faces away from the swimming pool.

2. Openings in the barrier should not allow the passage of a **4**-inch-diameter sphere.

3. Pedestrian access gates should open outward, away from the pool, and should have a(n) **self-latching** device.

Answer Key for Quiz 12

1. **pH** is the single most important element in a swimming pool's water chemistry..

2. If the pH is too **high**, the water becomes cloudy.

3. T/F: To avoid problems with water quality, pH must be maintained between 7.2 and 7.8.
   Answer: **True**

4. There aren't many significant differences between commercial and residential pools and spas; commercial pools and equipment are simply **bigger**.

5. T/F: Commercial pools use surge tanks.
   Answer: **True**

6. T/F: Signs are not required for commercial pools.
   Answer: **False**

H HOUSE OF HORRORS®

AN ENTIRE HOUSE. THOUSANDS OF DEFECTS. BUILT UNDER OUR ROOF.

BOULDER, COLORADO

WESTON, FLORIDA

EXPERT
HANDS-ON TRAINING

WRITE
THE BEST REPORTS

TEST-DRIVE
INSPECTION TOOLS

ELEVATE
YOUR BRAND

JOIN US FOR A LIVE CLASS AT THE HOUSE OF HORRORS®!

Visit www.nachi.org/training to view all of our upcoming classes and events!

INSPECTOR OUTLET

YOU'LL BE SHOCKED BY OUR LOW PRICES!

Inspector Outlet is your source for all things home inspection-related. We are the official store for InterNACHI® publications, equipment and apparel. We strive to provide the best products at the lowest prices in the industry.

InterNACHI® members get the best pricing on tools, testing equipment and meters.

Find an outstanding selection of original training manuals, checklists, articles and PDFs, as well as publications for clients, including the best-selling home maintenance guide, *Now That You've Had a Home Inspection*.

We offer a great line of protective outerwear and customized apparel for home inspectors, including shirts, jackets and hats.

InterNACHI's Inspector Marketing Department can design and print a variety of custom marketing materials for your home inspection business.

Protect yourself and your clients on the job with our specialized safety and inspection equipment that help make your inspections easier and safer.

Are you an InterNACHI® member? Inspector Outlet offers free inspector decals and embroidered patches to all eligible members!

"Inspector Outlet is officially endorsed by InterNACHI® for the best prices in the business for our members."
—Nick Gromicko, Founder of InterNACHI®

INSPECTOR OUTLET

www.InspectorOutlet.com   Sales@InspectorOutlet.com